RESUMES
THAT STAND OUT!

RESUMES
THAT STAND OUT!

TIPS FOR COLLEGE STUDENTS AND RECENT GRADS FOR WRITING
A SUPERIOR RESUME AND SECURING AN INTERVIEW

✔ Numerous examples of winning resumes to set you apart from the competition

✔ Simple-to-read instructions and proven frameworks—like a personal consultation

✔ Bonus chapters on writing influential cover letters and mastering a career fair so you can start interviewing

L. XAVIER CANO

Copyright © 2014 by Innovative Resume Consulting LLC.

Library of Congress Control Number: 2013922597
ISBN-13: 978-0692224625
ISBN-10: 0692224629

Chester Publishing

Legal disclaimer: Although the recommendations in this book have proven successful to a significant number of people, using these guidelines does not guarantee you will achieve success. The author and publisher shall in no event be held liable for any loss or other damages. Trust your own judgment when making decisions.

Trademarks: All brand names and product names used in this book are trade names, service marks, trademarks, or registered trademarks of their respective owners.

This book was printed in the United States of America.

To order additional copies of this book, contact:
Innovative Resume Consulting LLC
contact@TheInnovativeResume.com

CONTENTS

I dedicate this book to my family, the most important people in my life—my mom, Dr. Grisel Gómez-Cano, who taught me at an early age that I could accomplish anything as long as I worked hard and also for her invaluable feedback and time spent reviewing this book; my dad, Lorenzo Cano, who always reminds me of who I am and where I come from; my twin brother, Eduardo Cano, and his wife, Alma Cano; my sister, Yajaira Smith, for her many hours of editing services and support, and her husband, Drew Smith, for his insight; my sister, Xochitl Skibin, and her husband, Joshua Skibin, for their time reviewing this book; my nieces and nephews—Nyah, Ezra, America, Emily, Camila, Viviana, Gavin, Kayson, and Kaylin—whom I hope to inspire; my beautiful wife, soul mate, and best friend, María Reyes-Cano, who has supported me in all my endeavors and has shown me the true meaning of life; and finally, to my sweet daughter, Eva Sofía Cano, who has captivated my heart and soul.

Excellent book! Step-by-step manual that leaves no doubts on the reader's mind about what an outstanding resume should be. The author's personal experiences help the reader know exactly where the author is coming from and get a closer, more personal feel toward the text.

—Eleazar Zavala, junior, Texas State University

I feel that this book has given me the appropriate information I need to know to complete an outstanding resume. It was very well-explained with clear instructions on what to include and what not to include in a resume. The diagrams are easy to follow and provide great examples. All my questions about writing a professional resume were answered very well. I will definitely be using the tips and knowledge from this book to help me write future resumes. I will also highly recommend it to my college classmates.

—Ashley Olmeda, freshman, University of Mary Hardin-Baylor

This book provided me everything I needed to know about making my resume better than the rest. This how-to guide tells you what to include and what not to include with examples, but what I appreciated the most was his chapter on "Tips for Making the Most Out of a Career Fair". He lays out every step for you from preparation and research of the companies beforehand, when you should arrive at the career fair, and even why you should send a thank you letter to recruiters you met with. I know I will be more confident about attending a career fair now that I know what I should do.

—Brenton T. Raynor, junior, University of Houston—Downtown

An excellent, thorough, and informative professional development resource! I highly recommend this book to anyone looking to craft or improve his or her resume.

—Xochitl Skibin, graduate, University of Texas Medical Branch

This is one of my new favorite comprehensive resources essential for students and recent grads who need to know the intricacies of writing a professional resume. Filled with numerous tips and examples, it details section by section how a good resume should read.

—Adelina Longoria, affiliate faculty,
the Chicago School of Professional Psychology

L. Xavier Cano provides sound, thorough end-to-end direction to successfully outline your experience and education and increase your impact with employers and ultimately land interviews from your target companies or opportunities. Xavier's book is a valuable resource in any college student's or recent graduate's repertoire to attain his or her next ideal role.

—Carlos A. Fernandez, MBA, PHR, senior recruiter,
Houston Methodist

L. Xavier Cano does an excellent job in providing a step-by-step approach to building a resume visually from top to bottom. I found that this book would proactively answer questions as I read along. Through the various methods he uses to point to different formats and options for building a resume, Xavier does a great job in keeping the reader actively engaged. I highly recommend this book to anyone who is looking to build or update an impressionable and high-quality resume.

—Abraham Arevalo, graduate,
Leonard N. Stern School of Business

This is an outstanding book! It gives the reader a full spectrum on how to successfully land the most important meeting candidates should prepare for . . . the job interview. This is a must read for all applicants at any career level looking for better professional opportunities. Xavier provides practical and clear tips that can help make every candidate stand out.

—Annia L. Zavala, corporate vice president—recruiting,
New York Life Insurance Company

The succinct progression evolving from the statistical towards the personal while creating one's resume is a winning formula clearly spelled out by Cano. Despite Cano's emphasis on brevity, the intricacies and complexities involved in the process are not disregarded due to his constructive clarity. I wish I had such a guide when I first set out establishing my career path. For those already in careers and seeking to change, this guide contains information and suggestions to successfully jump-start those endeavors.

—Alex Horstman, owner and broker-in-charge,
Oak Realty LLC

This book is rewarding with each page and is a must read for all college students. Cano goes in-depth over everything that is needed from getting your cover letter in order to navigating and making a career fair work for you. Cano does a great job with his clear examples on what to think about before, during, and after a career fair to land that first interview. This book comes highly recommended for anyone who wants to equip themselves with the skills and knowledge to get that job easily.

—Asif Ahmad, Web Systems Engineer,
National Instruments

This book was brilliantly written and informative and the cartoons gave it a nice humorous touch. This book will answer all your questions about how to write a successful resume to impress your future employer.

—Kylie Pell, sophomore, Texas State University

After reading through the chapters on cover letter writing and mastering a career fair, I realized just how lost I would have been when it came time for me to write a cover letter or attend a career fair. Xavier Cano goes through the step-by-step details for what needs to be in each cover letter section, followed by examples of what a successful one should look like. It makes writing one seem ten times easier. Xavier Cano also explores every possible question anyone could have before attending a career fair and thoroughly explains every detail a prospective employee should take before, during, and after the career fair. If I ever attend one, I will be following all the tips this chapter gives in order to make the most of it.

—Erin Gogulski, freshman, Texas Christian University

This book really helped show me how to keep my resume short but effective and how to catch the recruiter's attention. Overall, I now know how to better my resume and to always keep an updated one on hand at all times!

—Tram Kim, RDMS, ultrasound technologist,
Texas Children's Hospital

Preface

I first became acquainted with my friend *the resume* as a sophomore at the University of Houston. Back then, he felt more like a nagging bully! It all began on a bright and early Monday morning.

It was almost 8:00 a.m. when my dad dropped me off at my college campus. I hated not having my own vehicle! I knew that with a summer internship, I could depend less on my parents. Either way, I arrived at my first class, which was taught by one of the teacher's assistants, a student in her senior year. She began to explain our assignment, to prepare a resume, and we only had a few days to construct it! I felt a punch in the stomach!

The first couple of days, I procrastinated writing my resume. When I finally gathered enough courage to get started, I had no idea where to begin and spent two hours staring at a blank screen. Was I supposed to include my middle name? What type of font should I use? Should I include my first job as a busboy? After many hours of stress and no product, I decided to write down all my accomplishments since kindergarten. I felt much better having something to turn in and thought I had done a decent job. Well, the teaching assistant had a different opinion. Let's just say that my original draft needed to be changed drastically! In fact, all the students had to alter theirs quite a bit.

It was then that I became more intrigued about resume writing. I thought that if this piece of paper could make the difference between having a good job and having my dad continue to drive me everywhere, I definitely needed to give it more attention! So that week, I visited the university career services center and picked up some information containing additional tips on resume writing. I learned important lessons such as how

I didn't need to include the fact that I won third place in a fourth grade science fair project!

For the rest of my sophomore year, I attended at least five more workshops held on and off campus and became very educated on the resume-writing process. I felt like I gained "inside knowledge" to write a winning resume and get hired by a top company! He was starting to feel less like a bully and more like a friend.

By my junior year, I had developed a resume-writing style and began coaching friends and colleagues on preparing their own resumes. I found myself helping a different person at least once a week. During my senior year, I led resume-writing workshops for the Program for Mastery in Engineering Studies (PROMES) at U of H and at regional conferences.

Once I graduated, I had the chance to review resumes for jobs we were looking to fill at the Dell manufacturing plant, which gave me additional understanding of what made certain resumes stand out from others. Also, I led workshops for the second-shift associates, roughly two hundred people. For the next few years, I continued coaching friends and colleagues, at least one person every other week, who had recently graduated from college and even friends applying for their master's degrees. Those around me began calling me *The Resume Whiz*. Since then, I formed a company called Innovative Resume Consulting LLC with the objective of coaching groups on resume writing and other professional development topics.

This book is written for undergraduate students and recent college graduates who are searching for an internship or job. The chapters that follow are simple to understand and provide many examples, so that you, my dear readers, will feel comfortable with the road ahead.

I still remember that stressful day during my sophomore year when I felt overwhelmed about the assignment. If you ever feel this way, just remember that writing a resume can be easy, and you will see why as you read the pages in this book!

Chapter 1

Introduction

Are you in one or more of the following situations?

- You are in a college class, and your professor has asked you to create a resume.
- You want to apply for a summer job or internship.
- You are trying to secure your first "real" job.
- You are not happy with your current position or just ready to move into a different role.
- You are trying to get ahead of the game by completing a crucial document that you will eventually need. (Good for you!)

If you answer yes, you are probably thinking, *How do I write a resume?* Well, don't panic. You are not alone, and you are in good hands.

In chapter 2, I will clarify common misconceptions regarding the purpose of the resume, provide you with a good definition, and illustrate the different sections.

Chapters 3 through 15 describe each resume section in greater detail, providing a thorough description of the components making up each section and tips and techniques that you can incorporate to make your resume stand out. In addition, I offer guidance for making aesthetic improvements.

In chapter 16, you will view examples of complete resumes to get a better idea of what winning resumes are supposed to look like. These incorporate the tips and techniques discussed in chapters 3 through 15.

I also added two bonus chapters to this book! Chapter 17 provides tips on how to create a cover letter, and chapter 18 will teach you how to make the most out of a career fair. You will learn many valuable tips in these two chapters.

I advise that you read this book from beginning to end since each subsequent chapter builds upon the previous one. Think of this experience as a personal session where I provide you with easy, step-by-step instructions to create your resume. By the time you finish, you will have all the knowledge to produce a superior resume that will impress that college professor, recruiter, and even yourself. You don't even have to shell out big bucks to do it!

Congratulations on taking the first step in preparing for a better future!

Chapter 2

What Is a Resume?

Before I provide you with a formal definition of the *resume*, we should clear up a common misconception about its purpose. Most people think that it is a document that is going to get them a job. However, this is not 100 percent true. The purpose of a resume is to impress a recruiter or hiring manager enough so that you are offered an *interview*. Let us repeat that.

> The purpose of a resume is to get you an interview, which could eventually lead you to getting a job offer.

What Is a Resume?

> A *resume* is a one-page document that summarizes your skills, work experience, and accomplishments.

You must have your resume available whenever you are ready to apply for an internship or job; therefore, it serves as a marketing tool. Company recruiters and/or hiring managers will review it and determine if you should receive an interview for the internship or job you are applying for. The stronger your resume is, the greater the chance that you will be invited for an interview. As you can see, having a great resume is crucial. And lucky for you, I am going to share with you several techniques that if used correctly will put you one hundred steps ahead of the competition.

What Goes In a Resume?

So what information should you include in your resume? You'll find that you may get a slightly different answer depending on whom you ask. In general, an undergraduate or recent grad's resume will consist of the following sections:

- The heading
- Career objective
- Education
- Work experience
- Skills (both technical and nontechnical)
- Awards/achievements/honors
- Extracurricular activities/leadership roles
- Languages spoken

Some additional (but optional) sections may include the following:

- Community involvement
- International travel
- Special projects
- Hobbies/interests

As we continue through the chapters, we'll go through each section in more detail. Let's get started!

Chapter 3

The Heading

The heading is the first section of your resume. It should contain your name, mailing address, phone number, and e-mail address. Let's go through each of these components in more detail.

Your Name

It is important to make your name stand out on the resume. Below are a few tips to do this:

- Center your name at the very top of the page.
- Make your name stand out by choosing a font size about 6 to 8 sizes larger than the font size of the rest of the resume (i.e., If you choose a font size of 12 for the body, then it would be appropriate to choose font size 18 or 20 for your name).
- List your name in bold font.
- Optional—you can capitalize each letter of your name.

Can I Use My Nickname?

Use your legal name rather than your nickname. For example, if your friends call you Lisa, Ben, or Chris but your legal name is Elizabeth, Benjamin, or Christopher respectively, then you would write Elizabeth Smith, not Lisa Smith; Benjamin Perez, not Ben Perez; or Christopher Adams, not Chris Adams. If you receive an interview, you can share with the recruiter or interviewer your preferred name when asked.

Should I Include My Middle Name?

If you go by your first name but you also have a middle name, you have the option to include your middle name or your middle initial. For example, if your name is Carlos Mario Rodriguez, you have the option of writing Carlos M. Rodriguez, Carlos Mario Rodriguez, or just Carlos Rodriguez. If you think you may have a common first and last name, I recommend you include your full middle name because it will eliminate any ambiguity if for any reason there is another resume being evaluated with a similar first and last name.

What If I Typically Go by My Middle Name?

If you go by your middle name instead of your first name, you should still include your full legal name. For example, if you have always gone by your middle name Mahla but your first name is Sireeta, you should write your full name on the resume as Sireeta Mahla Gupta.

Name Summary

To summarize, table 3.1 lists the different formats for including your name on the resume:

Table 3.1. How to write your name on your resume.

Format	Example
First Name, Last Name	Ariel Smith or ARIEL SMITH
First Name, Middle Name, Last Name	Ariel Karla Smith or ARIEL KARLA SMITH
First Name, Middle Initial, Last Name	Ariel K. Smith or ARIEL K. SMITH

Your Mailing Address

You should include a mailing address where you are comfortable receiving mail, especially from a company that may be interested in interviewing you. For example, many students have a home address but also have a dorm address if they live on campus. Which one should you use?

> Use the mailing address where you expect to receive information in the event that a company sends you a letter.

I have heard stories of people who included a mailing address that was not current, and as a result, they did not receive the important documents sent by the employers.

When writing the mailing address, include the city, state, and zip code. Do not abbreviate any parts of the address such as street, lane, boulevard, drive, circle, court, etc. For example, "4800 Long Meadow St." should be written in the resume as "4800 Long Meadow Street."

Your Phone Number

Make sure that you include a phone number where you can be reached. For example, some people may have a landline where they live and may also have a cell phone. I recommend providing your cell phone number instead of your landline so that if a recruiter calls you, you have quicker access to the call.

I have met people who wrote their home phone number on the resume instead of their cell phone number. When recruiters called, their mom, grandma, or significant other answered the phone. In one case, the mother did not speak English and could not determine who was calling her son and for what purpose. As a result, the student later found out that he missed an opportunity to be interviewed with a company. Therefore, it is important to have a phone number listed that will increase the probability of having recruiters reach you if they call.

Your Voice Mail Recording

There are situations when you may not be available to pick up calls on your cell phone. Perhaps you are in class, in a meeting, or just in an area where the reception is poor. In these cases, the recruiter may leave you a voice mail. This is okay. However, my advice is to make sure your voice mail recording is clean and professional. The following voice mail recording would be very appropriate:

> *"Hello, you have reached the voice mail of Quincy Chang. I am unable to answer the phone at this moment, but please leave your name, number, and a short message, and I will return your call as soon as possible."*

The worst thing you can do is have a voice mail that sounds unprofessional. For example, you should remove any obnoxious music from the background and any inappropriate words. One recruiter told me that she called a student who had a voice mail where vulgar language was used. That student lost the opportunity to be interviewed for this company.

In addition, students may have voice mails that are clean but may sound juvenile. For example, a recruiter told me that one student had a creative voice mail, pretending to be answering the phone, but then said, "Just kidding! Tricked you! I'm not here. Please call me later." The recruiter chose not to interview this student because she felt the voice mail recording was immature.

© 2004 Ted Goff

Goff

"Don't worry. I have your resume right in front of me."

Your E-mail Address

You should create a professional e-mail address that is used for business purposes only, and it should be kept simple and contain your first name and last name and, if possible, be separated by either a period (.) or underscore (_). This is the e-mail address you will use on your resume. See formats and examples below in table 3.2:

Table 3.2. How to write your e-mail address on your resume.

Format	Example
FirstnameLastname@domainname.com	RubenArmstrong@mail.com
Firstname.Lastname@domainname.com	Ruben.Armstrong@mail.com
Firstname_Lastname@domainname.com	Ruben_Armstrong@mail.com

What If My Professional E-mail Address Is Already Taken by Someone Else?

If you have a very common first and last name, you may find that your professional e-mail address may already be taken by someone else. If this is the case, include your middle name or middle initial or a few numbers in your e-mail address. For example, *Ruben.B.Armstrong@mail.com* or *Ruben.Armstrong2001@mail.com* would be appropriate. Please note that I would not recommend including more than four numbers in your e-mail address. You can also abbreviate your first and/or middle name if needed but never your last name.

The following e-mail addresses would also be appropriate on a resume *if needed*:

- *Ruben.Bryan.Armstrong@mail.com*
- *Ruben.Armstrong2001@mail.com*

- *R_Armstrong@mail.com*
- *RBArmstrong@mail.com*
- *RBArmstrong23@mail.com*

Can My E-mail Address Offend a Recruiter?

Believe it or not, the e-mail address you choose can offend a recruiter if it contains language or words that are unprofessional or juvenile. To give you an idea, table 3.3 illustrates e-mail addresses that may be seen as inappropriate or juvenile to recruiters, which may cause them to stop reading your resume.

Table 3.3. Inappropriate e-mail addresses for a resume.

Examples of E-mail Addresses Not to Use	Reasoning
Unicorn12324@mail.com	Using the word *unicorn* may sound inappropriate. The person's name does not appear in this e-mail address. There are more than four numbers listed.
Nate.Jones@mail.com	The person's first name is actually Nathan, which should have been used instead of the nickname Nate.
Daniel@mail.com	The person's last name does not appear in this e-mail address.
1002038dasd@mail.com	The person's name does not appear in this e-mail address. There are more than four numbers listed.

Should My E-mail Address Be Underlined and Written in Blue Font?

When typing your e-mail address, some word processing programs will turn it into a hyperlink, meaning that it will appear underlined and in blue font. This is okay if you will be sending your resume electronically but not desirable if you will be physically submitting it or mailing it. If you are printing your resume, highlight the e-mail address and turn the hyperlink function off so that it does not appear as a hyperlink.

The Heading Layout

Now let's take a look at how the name, address, phone number, and e-mail address should appear on the resume. Figs. 3-1 and 3-2 demonstrate two different heading layouts, and figs. 3-3 and 3-4 are corresponding examples. Feel free to use one or the other. Typically, heading layout 2 is used whenever you need a few more lines to completely fill one page.

> # First Name Middle Name Last Name
>
> *address (street number and street name)*   *phone number*
> *address (city, state, and zip code)*   *e-mail address*

Figure 3-1. Heading layout 1.

First Name Middle Name Last Name

address (street number and street name)
address (city, state, and zip code)
phone number
e-mail address

Figure 3-2. Heading layout 2.

Ruben Bryan Armstrong

4800 Long Meadow Street   *704.345.6789*
Charlotte, NC 23456   *Ruben.Armstrong@mail.com*

Figure 3-3. Example using heading layout 1.

Ruben Bryan Armstrong

4800 Long Meadow Street
Charlotte, NC 23456
704.345.6789
Ruben.Armstrong@mail.com

Figure 3-4. Example using heading layout 2.

I recommend that the mailing address, phone number, and e-mail address have a font 1 size smaller than the font size of the actual content of the resume (i.e., if you choose a font size of 12 for the content, then choose a font size of 11 for the mailing address, phone number, and e-mail address).

I also recommend italicizing the address, phone number, and e-mail address. In my opinion, it will give your resume a cleaner and more professional look.

Should I Include My LinkedIn® URL?

Nowadays, more and more recruiters are using LinkedIn to learn about prospective job candidates. Include your LinkedIn URL on your resume in the heading right under the e-mail address only if your LinkedIn profile is complete, your LinkedIn URL has been customized, your picture looks professional, and you have additional items to showcase not present in your resume.

The next chapter will discuss how you can immediately start impressing recruiters with your career objective.

Chapter 4

Career Objective

The career objective is the next section of the resume and is located at the top of the page right below the heading. It consists of one or two sentences, which answer the following questions:

1. **What industry do you want to work in** (e.g., fashion, oil & gas, or telecommunications)?

2. **What position do you want to have within this industry** (e.g., designer, engineer, or accountant)?

A well thought-out career objective informs recruiters of your specific career interests and, indirectly, sends the message that you are a serious candidate. Unfortunately, most people make the mistake of including a career objective that is too general. For example, what do you think about the following?

Looking for a job in a top corporation that will allow me to utilize my skills

While this sample career objective may be an honest statement, it does not specify the position or industry that the applicant is interested in. This will lead the recruiter to believe that the applicant is not sure of what he or she wants to do. Companies want to recruit individuals who have a strong idea of what they are seeking, so answering the two questions provided earlier as part of the career objective is very important. The following is a better one:

> *Looking for a <u>management position</u> within the <u>pharmaceutical industry</u> that will allow me to utilize my skills*

> *(Note: Do not underline any words in the career objective. I did this above so that you could see the "buzz" words.)*

This career objective is more effective because it allows the recruiter to understand what type of role and industry the person is interested in. However, you also have the option to add a few more items to market yourself even further. Please read on.

Addition of Self-descriptors and Skills in the Career Objective

There is still room to add a few more items that will make the career objective more impressive such as including a few effective adjectives to describe your personal, intellectual, and technical skills. Keep in mind that this is one of the first sections the recruiter or hiring manager is going to read. What do you think of the following career objective?

> *<u>Self-motivated</u> and <u>honest</u> individual with <u>strong leadership</u> and <u>organizational</u> skills looking for a <u>management position</u> within the <u>pharmaceutical</u> industry*

Immediately, we can see that this career objective stands out more than the original one. *(Reminder: Do not underline any words in the career objective. I did this in the previous example so that you could see the "buzz" words.)*

So with that said, the following are a few good frameworks to create your career objective. The first set of adjectives describes your positive traits, and the second set describes your functional skills useful for the desired position. Fill in the sections within the brackets.

Career Objective Framework 1

[*Adjective*] and [*adjective*] <u>*student*</u> with [*adjective*] and [*adjective*] skills <u>*interested in*</u> a [*function*] <u>*position*</u> within the [*industry type*] industry

Below is another great example of a winning career objective using this framework:

> <u>*Positive*</u> and <u>*energetic*</u> student with <u>*mathematical*</u> and <u>*computer*</u> skills interested in an <u>*accounting*</u> position within the <u>*consumer packaged goods*</u> industry

In the framework, feel free to replace a few of the underlined words with alternate ones as stated in table 4.1, taking into consideration the grammar rules.

Table 4.1. Framework alternate words

Framework Word(s) Examples	Alternate Framework Word(s) Examples
student	undergraduate, leader, college graduate, individual, etc.
interested in	seeking, looking for, searching for, pursuing, etc.
position	internship, job, opportunity, career, role, etc.

Please note that not all jobs are industrial in nature. These typically include teachers, professors, counselors, and social workers. In these cases, you would leave out the last part of the career objective framework that makes reference to the industry. If you are interested in a role as a teacher, professor, or social worker, use Career Objective Framework 2:

Career Objective Framework 2

[*Adjective*] and [*adjective*] *student* with [*adjective*] and [*adjective*] skills *interested in* a [*function*] *position*

The following is a sample career objective using Career Objective Framework 2:

Responsible and *supportive* individual with *great interpersonal* and *speaking* skills pursuing a *mental health counselor* position

Below is another example:

Smart and *productive* graduate with *superb leadership* and *facilitation* skills seeking a *middle-school teacher* position

For your convenience, below is a short list of the many adjectives available that would be appropriate to include in your career objective, whether you use framework 1 or 2. You can use them to describe yourself or some of the skills you have. As stated earlier, please take into consideration the grammar rules when choosing adjectives.

Personality-related adjectives (e.g., *positive and energetic student*)

- accomplished
- accountable
- acute
- clear
- clever
- collaborative
- compassionate
- competent
- adaptable
- admirable
- advanced
- expert
- extraordinary
- flexible
- fruitful
- gifted
- brilliant
- capable
- cheerful
- proficient
- prolific
- proven
- quick
- reliable

- confident
- cooperative
- cosmopolitan
- creative
- curious
- dependable
- determined
- diverse
- dynamic
- eager
- effective
- efficient
- energetic
- enthusiastic
- ethical
- excellent
- exceptional
- excited
- experienced
- well-organized
- global
- helpful
- honest
- industrious
- ingenious
- innovative
- intelligent
- inventive
- investigative
- knowledgeable
- logical
- loyal
- methodical
- outstanding
- passionate
- perceptive
- positive
- productive
- professional
- resourceful
- responsible
- self-motivated
- sharp
- sincere
- skilled
- smart
- sophisticated
- strategic
- superb
- superior
- supportive
- systematic
- talented
- trustworthy
- upbeat
- vibrant
- well-developed

Skills-related adjectives (e.g., *mathematical and computer skills)*

(Note: Although the words listed below are not in their stand-alone adjective form, you can place them in front of the word *skills*.)

- active listening
- analytical
- communication
- computer
- coordination
- critical thinking
- measurement
- memorization
- great multitasking
- decision making
- environment awareness
- forecasting
- editing
- information finding
- presentation
- print design
- problem solving
- programming
- information technology
- interpersonal
- leadership
- marketing
- mathematical
- speaking
- technical
- time management
- typography

- negotiation
- networking
- operation monitoring
- organization
- persuasion

- project management
- reading comprehension
- service orientation

- web design
- writing

More work-related skills and examples are provided in chapter 7.

Below, you can see how the career objective would look like in the partial resume in fig. 4-1:

Ruben Bryan Armstrong

4800 Long Meadow Street
Charlotte, NC 23456

704.345.6789
Ruben.Armstrong@mail.com

Career Objective: Dynamic and innovative student with exceptional analytical and modeling skills searching for an industrial engineering role within the airline industry

---

Figure 4-1. Partial resume with an example of a career objective.

What Should I Do If I Do Not Know What Type of Position I Am Looking for or What Industry I Am Interested in? (IMPORTANT)

Many students are not sure of their future professional plans prior to starting college or even while taking college classes. The most important step is to get on a track that will unfold as the collegiate experience unfolds. Below is my rule:

> *If you do not know what role or industry you want to work in, go ahead and leave the career objective section blank for now. Then whenever you want to apply for a job, fill out the career objective section with the corresponding role and industry.*

If you have to write a resume for a specific class and therefore cannot leave the career objective blank, don't sweat it. Just pick a job that you think you might be interested in and formulate your career objective around it. It's that simple.

If you are interested in applying for different roles and/or industries at the same time, **it is important that you create resumes with different career objectives for each position you are applying for.** For example, let's say that you are applying for roles in project management for a company in the oil and gas industry and one in the computer hardware industry, your career objective will look slightly different.

Below is an example of a career objective for an internship in the oil and gas industry:

> *Ethical and perceptive undergraduate with excellent coordinating and negotiating skills searching for a project management internship within the oil and gas industry*

Below is a career objective for an internship in the computer hardware industry:

> *Ethical and perceptive undergraduate with excellent coordinating and negotiating skills searching for a project management internship within the computer hardware industry*

In this day and age where competition for work is fierce, it is more impressive for recruiters to read in your resume a career objective that clearly and specifically illustrates the role and industry you are interested in. Remember, the career objective is the first section a recruiter is going to see. Make it count!

Industries

For your reference, a list of industries you may be interested in working for is provided below:

- Accounting
- Advertising
- Aerospace
- Agriculture
- Aircraft
- Airline
- Automotive
- Biotechnology and pharmaceuticals
- Broadcasting
- Computer hardware
- Computer software
- Consulting
- Consumer products
- Cosmetics
- Defense
- Education
- Electronics
- Energy
- Fashion
- Financial services and insurance
- Food and beverage
- Government and politics
- Grocery
- Health care
- Investment banking
- Legal
- Management consulting
- Manufacturing
- Media and entertainment
- Newspaper publishers
- Nonprofit/social services
- Oil and gas
- Pension funds

- Private equity
- Publishing
- Real estate
- Securities and commodities exchanges
- Service
- Soap and detergent
- Software
- Sports
- Technology
- Telecommunications
- Transportation
- Utilities
- Venture capital

The resume's education section will be discussed in the next chapter.

© 2010 Ted Goff

"A very impressive resume.
I really like your career goal
of ruling the world."

Chapter 5

Education

The education section of a resume includes specific information about your educational background. It typically comes after the career objective section and should include two to three lines of information. The following components should be included:

- The name of the college or university you attend or attended
- The name of the school within the university or college you attend or attended
- The city and state of the college or university
- Your graduation date (tentative or actual)
- Your degree (major)
- Your minor (optional)
- Your GPA (optional)
- Special accomplishments (optional)

Fig. 5-1 is an example of a partial resume and the education section:

Ruben Bryan Armstrong

4800 Long Meadow Street
Charlotte, NC 23456

704.345.6789
Ruben.Armstrong@mail.com

Career Objective: Dynamic and innovative student with exceptional analytical and modeling skills searching for an industrial engineering position in the airline industry

Education

The University of Houston, Cullen College of Engineering   Houston, TX   **GPA:** 3.75
Bachelor of Science in Industrial Engineering   Expected May 2014

- Industrial Engineering Senior of the Year 2014

Figure 5-1. Partial resume illustrating the education section.

The following are a few tips to make the best use of the components making up the education section.

College or University

- Ensure that the **formal name of the university** appears on the resume just as it would appear on your diploma.
- Do NOT abbreviate the name of your college or university.

Table 5.1 illustrates appropriate versus inappropriate ways to present the name of your college or university in the education section.

Table 5.1. Examples of appropriately-named colleges.

Appropriate	Inappropriate
The University of Texas at Austin	UT
The University of Pennsylvania	Univ. of Pennsylvania
The University of Houston OR The University of Houston-Central Campus	U of H
Sam Houston State University	Sam Houston State
Rice University	Rice
University of Mississippi	Ole Miss
Massachusetts Institute of Technology	MIT

School within the College or University

- Spell out the school's name within the college or university you attend next to the name of the university.
- You can separate the university's name from the school's name by using a comma or a hyphen.

Below are a few examples:

- *The University of Texas at Austin, McCombs School of Business*
- *The University of Houston-Cullen College of Engineering*
- *The University of Houston-Central Campus, College of Technology*
- *Sam Houston State University-College of Humanities and Social Sciences*
- *Rice University, The Shepherd School of Music*
- *The University of California-Berkeley, School of Public Health*

City and State

You should include the city and state of the college or university you attend.

Regarding the city and state, sometimes people are not sure if they should abbreviate the state name. For example, should you write Charlotte, *NC*, or Charlotte, *North Carolina*? Below is my general rule:

> *If there IS enough room in the resume to spell out the full name of the state without making the section look cluttered, then spell it out. If there IS NOT enough room, then it is okay to abbreviate the state name in all caps.*

GPA

A question frequently asked is if a GPA should be included on the resume. My general rule is as follows:

> *If your GPA is 3.0 (out of 4.0) or higher, then include it on the resume. If your GPA is NOT 3.0 or higher, then do NOT include it on the resume.*

If you ask others for advice on this question, they may tell you to always include your GPA because recruiters and hiring managers will ask you for it before they can offer you an interview. However, I disagree with this statement. If your GPA is lower than 3.0, it is considered a red flag for a lot of recruiters. As a result, many may choose not to interview you. However, as we all know, a GPA only tells part of the story.

You may have a lower GPA not necessarily because you did not do well overall in school. Perhaps you were extremely involved with campus extracurricular activities or maybe you worked or are working part-time to pay for tuition or maybe you had a personal tragedy that caused you to do poorly on a few tests that resulted in you having a lower GPA.

The point is that if you leave out a GPA that is lower than 3.0 and a recruiter sees your resume and is impressed with everything else you have included on it, the recruiter may not request your GPA and may give you the interview regardless. So my advice is to leave out your GPA if it is lower than 3.0 and always include it if it is 3.0 or higher.

A key point I want to emphasize is that it is important to study appropriately so that you can have the best GPA possible, which will always look better on the resume and increase the chances of you receiving an interview.

Should I Include My Major GPA or Cumulative GPA?

A major GPA is a grade point average that only takes into consideration the grades received in classes specific toward your major (not the classes you take to fulfill your basics). A cumulative GPA takes into consideration the grades you received in all your classes. Always include the higher GPA. However, if the major GPA is the higher of the two, then write the word *major* next to the grade point average that you listed. For example, if your major GPA is 3.5 and your cumulative GPA is 3.1, use the higher of the two, which in this case is the major GPA of 3.5. Your GPA should appear on your resume as follows: GPA: 3.5 (major).

Your Major

When reviewing resumes, some people write their degree major by only listing the discipline. There is nothing wrong with this practice. However, the following tips will make your resume look more professional:

- Write the name of the degree you are pursuing instead of your major.
- Do *not* abbreviate the words in your degree *if* you have enough space to spell it out.

Table 5.2 below shows appropriate ways to include your degree:

Table 5.2. How to write your degree on the resume.

Preferred	Nonpreferred
Bachelor of Science in Industrial Engineering	Engineering
Bachelor of Science in Mechanical Engineering	Mechanical engineering
Bachelor of Arts in Marketing	Marketing
Bachelor of Arts in Finance	Major: finance
Bachelor of Science in Business Administration	Business
Bachelor of Arts in Music	BA in music
Bachelor of Science in Chemistry	B.S. in chemistry
Bachelor of Arts in Communication	Communication

Your Minor

You do not have to list a minor on your resume. If you decide to do so, then it can be listed simply as follows:

- *Minor: Russian*
- *Minor: Physics*
- *Minor: Mathematics*

Capitalize the word *minor* and the discipline (e.g., capitalize *Spanish* and *Finance* and *Statistics*).

Should I Include My Minor If It Is Very Different from My Major or Different from the Position I Am Applying For?

Some students have a minor in a discipline that is not related to the job or industry they are pursuing or just different from their major. When determining if you should include your minor, my recommendation is as follows:

> *If there is enough room on the resume to include a minor without creating clutter, then include it.*

Even though someone with a minor in music, dance, or anthropology may have majored in a field of study such as business or engineering, including the minor's discipline shows diversity of interests. For example, I received a Bachelor of Science degree in industrial engineering and a minor in music performance on flute from the University of Houston. Having this minor on my resume has always been a great conversation-starter at past interviews. So if your minor fits in the resume cleanly, I recommend you include it.

Graduation Date

If you have not graduated yet, then you can simply place the words *Tentative* or *Expected* preceding the month and year you expect to graduate. Refer to the following examples:

- *Tentative May 2015* or
- *Expected* 05/2015

If you are a recent graduate, list the month and year of your graduation date as follows:

- *May 2015 or*
- *05/2015*

In situations where you may have attended one university and then transferred to another one, another approach you can take is to list the range of months and/or years you attended each university. Please see examples below:

- *2011-2015* or
- *August 2011-May 2015* or
- *Aug. 2011-May 2015*

Should I Include the Junior College, Technical School, or Community College Where I Took a Few Classes or Where I Earned My Associate Degree?

- If you are still attending a junior college/technical school/ community college because you are working toward your associate degree, then include this information in the education section of the resume.
- If you are working on your bachelor's degree at a four-year college or university and you have taken a few classes at a junior college, you do *not* need to include the junior college/technical school/community college.
- If you are working on your bachelor's degree at a four-year college or university but you have an associate degree from a junior college, you have the option to list it as long as you have enough room on your resume.

Should I Include My Bachelor's Degree or Associate Degree First?

Keeping in mind the tips recommended earlier, if you choose to include your associate degree and your bachelor's degree, you should list each degree in reverse chronological order. For example, if you received an associate degree from a junior college and have either received a bachelor's degree or are working on completing your bachelor's degree at a university, you should list the bachelor's degree before the associate's degree. Please see example below:

EDUCATION

The University of North Dakota, College of Arts and Sciences   Grand Forks, ND   2011-2013
Bachelor of Arts in Sociology   Minor: Management   **GPA: 3.35**

Houston Community College-Southeast Campus   Houston, Texas   2009-2011
Associate of Arts in Social Science   **GPA: 4.0**

What If I Have a Double Major?

Below are a few tips on how to list a double major on the resume:

- If you have a double major, you should list each degree in the education section.
- If your two degrees came from the same school in the university, you do not need to list the school twice.
- If the two degrees came from different schools in the university, then you should list both schools.
- You can choose to include the words *dual degree* or not.

Please see examples below:

Example 1

EDUCATION

Texas A&M University, College of Liberal Arts   College Station, TX   Expected May 2016
Dual degree: Bachelor of Science in Economics and Bachelor of Arts in History   **GPA: 3.55**

OR

EDUCATION

Texas A&M University, College of Liberal Arts   College Station, TX   Expected May 2016
Bachelor of Science in Economics and Bachelor of Arts in History   **GPA: 3.55**

Example 2

Texas A&M University, College of Liberal Arts and Mays Business School   College Station, TX
Bachelor of Science in Economics and Bachelor of Science in Finance   Expected 05/16   **GPA: 3.1**

Special Educational Accomplishments

Later in the book, we are going to discuss the resume's awards section. In the event that you do not have enough room on the resume to include an awards or accomplishments section, feel free to include one or two big awards as part of the education section. Below are a few examples:

Example 1

Education
The University of Minnesota, College of Liberal Arts   Minneapolis, Minnesota
Bachelor of Science in Psychology   Expected December 2014   **GPA: 3.89**
Junior of the Year 2013

Example 2

EDUCATION

Rice University, George R. Brown School of Engineering   Houston, Texas   2009-2013
Bachelor of Science in Civil Engineering   **GPA: 3.77**
The XYZ Scholarship recipient; ABC Scholar; Sophomore of the Year 2010

Also, it is okay to list a brief description of an award (one sentence or phrase) if it is not obvious what the award is. In our example above, Sophomore of the Year is pretty self-explanatory. However, the XYZ Scholarship recipient and ABC Scholar are not. See below for an example:

EDUCATION

Rice University, George R. Brown School of Engineering   Houston, Texas   2009-2013
Bachelor of Science in Civil Engineering   **GPA: 3.77**
The XYZ Scholarship recipient (awarded for outstanding service to the community), ABC Scholar (awarded for making all As during freshman year), Sophomore of the Year 2010

Other Items to Take into Consideration

You have the option to italicize or set in boldface any of the components in the education section. I would recommend placing only the university, school, and GPA in bold font. The next section will discuss how to list your work experience.

© 2002 Ted Goff

"Just where is Quadrant-3 University?"

Chapter 6

Work Experience

Employers value potential job candidates who have prior experience in their particular field of work. Even so, recruiters understand that undergraduates are not going to have very many years in the labor force. Therefore, if you have work experience, this is your opportunity to show the recruiter the skills you possess. If you have never been employed, we will discuss in the next chapters how you can incorporate other types of skills you have gained in non-work-related situations.

This chapter will help you present your work experience and effectively highlight the skills you learned. The work experience section of a resume typically appears after the education segment. This section should include your current employment, internships obtained during college, and any part-time or full-time jobs held in the past or while going to school. For example, if you worked twenty hours a week or more as a bank teller or perhaps as an administrative assistant for an engineering firm, then this is the section where you would include this work experience.

Each job listed needs to have the following components:

- Company's full name
- Job title held
- Dates of employment
- City and state of employment
- Job duties (we will elaborate on this further)

Please note that you should list these elements for each individual job you have held, including your present one. To give you a better idea, fig. 6-1 provides an example of a partial resume showing how the work experience section should appear. Notice how the components are laid out for *each* job.

PETER ALEXANDER DANIELIAN

9999 Stonelake Boulevard
Orlando, FL 23456
876-345-6789
Peter.Danielian@mail.com

Career Objective

Friendly and professional finance undergraduate with problem solving and interpersonal communication skills looking for a finance position in the telecommunications industry

Education

University of Central Florida, College of Business Administration   Orlando, FL
Bachelor of Arts in Finance   Minor: Management   Expected May 2016   GPA: 3.35

Work Experience

Computer World Inc.   Naples, FL   August 2014-August 2015
Finance Assistant
- Collaborated with members of the finance team to assess proper reconciliation of accounts
- Demonstrated strong technical skills when utilizing internal databases to create monthly financial reports
- Reduced customer complaints by 25% by preparing work instructions to a key customer-facing process
- Collected weekly data for finance manager to enhance revenue of product base

Phone Land LLC   Miami, FL   June 2013-August 2014
Management Assistant
- Conducted credit history reviews to evaluate and approve new accounts
- Exemplified teamwork when coordinating customer questions with sales representatives
- Eliminated costs by 10% by creating daily reconciliation process

Figure 6-1. Partial resume with two jobs listed.

Now that you have seen how the work experience section fits into the resume, let's discuss each component in more detail.

Company's Full Name

You may have worked or are currently working for a company, nonprofit organization, college or school, or other government agency. You should start the work experience section by indicating the company/agency's full name. For example, let's say you have worked or are currently working for one of the following organizations:

- Chips and Dips Corporation
- Computer World XYZ Inc.
- Technology Products LLC
- The University of Xavier
- John Doe, DDS
- Uplifted Spirits Community Organization
- The City of Arcadia

The first column in table 6.1 shows the appropriate way of writing the company's name.

Table 6.1. Preferred and nonpreferred way to write the company's name.

Preferred	Nonpreferred
Chips and Dips Corporation	Chips and Dips
Computer World XYZ Inc.	Computer World XYZ
Technology Products LLC	Technology Products
The University of Xavier	UX
John Doe, DDS	John Doe
Uplifted Spirits Community Organization	USCO
The City of Arcadia	Arcadia

Job Title

List the name of positions held while working at each company. The job title will provide the recruiter a better idea of what function you played within the company. For example, the following are a few random job titles:

- Materials Intern
- Communications Intern
- Financial Advisor
- Dental Assistant
- Account Executive
- Bank Teller
- Office Assistant
- Event Planner
- Public Affairs Assistant
- Customer Service Representative

What If I Cannot Remember My Job Title?

If you cannot remember your previous job title, you can try a few things to find it:

- Look for any documents you may still have from your old employer containing your past title.
- Check if your past location of employment has a website. If so, search in the careers section for any positions that sound similar to what you had.
- Contact your old manager (if you feel comfortable doing this) and ask him or her for your past title.

If none of these tips help, then I would go ahead and create a title for that job, describing in a few words what you did. Table 6.2 contains a few examples:

Table 6.2. Rationale for determining job titles.

Title Created	Rationale
Warehouse Intern	You may have worked in a warehouse as an intern doing various tasks one summer.
Community Development Assistant	Perhaps you worked for a nonprofit organization for a semester doing community-development-type work.
Sales Assistant	You worked in a sales-related role for a company.
Engineering Intern	You assisted engineers in various tasks.
Communications Assistant	You may have worked in the communications department of a corporation assisting one of the executive managers.
Public Relations Intern	Perhaps you worked for a public relations firm one year as an intern.

As long as you do not exaggerate your title, it is okay to create one that uses one to three words describing what you did. The following titles in table 6.3 would *NOT* be appropriate as they are exaggerated or appear completely made-up given the function you performed.

Table 6.3. Inappropriately named job titles.

Title Created—NOT Appropriate	Function You Actually Performed
CEO	You may have worked in a warehouse as an intern doing various tasks one summer.
Executive Director	Perhaps you worked for a nonprofit organization for a semester doing community development type work.
Chief Sales Officer	You worked in a sales-related role under various supervisors
Vice President of Engineering	Perhaps you worked as an intern for an engineering company.
Sales Manager	You may have worked in the communications department of a corporation assisting one of the executive managers.
President	Perhaps you worked for a public relations firm one year as an intern.

© 2000 Ted Goff

"How long were you the Decision Enhancement Coordinator for the Acme Company Janitorial Department?"

Employment Dates

Employment dates should be listed for each job performed so that the recruiter can get a better idea of the length of time you held in each one. Any of the formats in the following table can be used for this purpose. You would typically include only the month and year that you started and ended your job. The first column in table 6.4 shows the format and the second shows a few examples.

Table 6.4. Format for dates of employment.

Format	Example
Month and year	March 2014-February 2015 or March 2014 to February 2015
Abbreviated month and year	Mar. 2014-Feb. 2015 or Mar. 2014 to Feb. 2015
Numeric month and the year's last two digits	03/14-02/15 or 03/14 to 02/15 or 3/14-2/15 or 3/14 to 2/15
Year(s) listed only	2006-2007 or 2006 to 2007

As you can see from the examples in the table, it is not Necessary to include the actual day you started and ended. Also, if you have extra room on the resume *and* it does not look cluttered, I would recommend choosing the option from the table where the months are spelled out completely. Likewise, if you find yourself fighting for room on the resume, use the shorter version of the month and year so that you have room on the resume to put more significant items.

What If I Only Worked for a Few Weeks or a Few Days at a Certain Company?

If you happened to do some type of internship or activity that only lasted for a few weeks or a few days, you can simply put the month and the year as well. See below:

- March 2014 or
- Mar. 2014 or
- 03/2014

What If I Am Still in My Current Position?

If you are still employed at an organization or are currently working, you should list the month and/or year when you started your current job followed by the word *present*. See table 6.5 below for some examples:

Table 6.5. Format for employment dates of current job.

Format	Example
Month and year	March 2013-present or March 2013 to present
Abbreviated month and year	Mar. 2013-present or Mar. 2013 to present
Numeric month and the last two digits of the year	03/13-present or 03/13 to present or 3/13-present or 3/13 to present
Year(s) listed only	2013-present or 2013 to present

City and State of Employment

You want to include the city and state of where you physically worked. Do not include the company's headquarter city and state unless you actually worked there. For example, if you worked in Encino, California, then you would put Encino, California, even though the main headquarters are in Houston, Texas.

What If I Worked in Different Cities for the Same Company?

If your experience involved working in different cities, then include all of them. For example, one summer, I collected data for Continental Airlines. My job involved spending four weeks in Houston, Texas; four weeks in Newark, New Jersey; and two weeks in Cleveland, Ohio. In this case, I would include these three cities as follows: Houston, Texas; Newark, New Jersey; Cleveland, Ohio.

Should I Spell Out the Names of the States Where I Worked?

It is your decision to spell out the names of the states where you worked as long as you show consistency throughout the work experience section. This means that if you spell out the name of the state where one of your jobs was located, then you need to spell out the names of the states where all your jobs were located as well. If this is going to cause any type of clutter, then I would recommend abbreviating the state names.

Job Duties

The job duties portion is not only the most important part of the work experience section but also of the entire resume because it is where you highlight what you did, the skills you gained, and contributions you made in each position. My recommendations will make your job duties section look more professional and increase your chances of being interviewed.

Most people tend to include *what* they did (their job duties), but they forget to include what they learned, skills they gained, or the difference they made for the company. Including these additional items is crucial because it will give the recruiter a deeper understanding of your strengths and what you could bring to the table.

For example, let's say that you write the following as one of the bullets in the work experience section:

- *Created a training manual on the usage of new scanners*

This is a good start because it highlights something you did in a past role. If the recruiter is looking for someone who has experience in creating training manuals and some knowledge of scanners or other similar devices, then this bullet is fine. However, I can also include in this bullet what I learned and the skills I gained or how I made a difference in the company. See the following two approaches:

Approach 1: *Mention what you learned and/or skills gained*

Using our previous example, the three bullets that follow will provide additional information on *what* you learned and/or skills gained:

- *Gained valuable cross-functional communication skills when creating a training manual on the usage of new scanners*

OR

- *Learned optimal bargaining strategies to interact with vendors when creating a training manual on the usage of new scanners*

OR

- *Became proficient at analyzing key process steps when creating a training manual on the usage of new scanners*

You can see that the information in these bullets provides more depth into what you did because it shows **what you learned and or skills gained**. The original bullet was fine and explained what was done, but the sample bullets used in approach 1 provide the recruiter additional information about your transferrable skills and experiences.

Approach 2: *Mention how you made a difference*

Using our original example, the three bullets that follow will provide additional information on how you made a difference:

- *Educated 300+ associates by creating a training manual on the usage of new scanners*

OR

- *Eliminated defects in the main assembly line by creating a training manual on the usage of new scanners*

OR

- <u>Increased productivity at the warehouse</u> by creating a training manual on the usage of new scanners

As you can see, the original bullet was fine, but these three bullets are stronger because they show **how** **you made a difference** in addition to what you did. The recruiter will see these accomplishments as proof of your problem-solving skills, which are valuable to any company. *(For your convenience, I underlined specific words in the examples above. However, do not underline these words on your resume).*

Structuring Your Bullets

To help you structure your sentences using the two approaches described, I provide you with the useful frameworks listed below.

Framework 1

If describing approach 1 (*what* you learned and/or skills gained), structure your sentence in the following format:

- Include what you learned or skill gained
- Connect by using the word *when*
- List the action performed (verb ending in *-ing*)

Example

Before

- *Ran billing and payroll for the bank*

After

- *Paid close attention to detail <u>when</u> runn<u>ing</u> billing and payroll for the bank*

Framework 2

If describing approach 2 (*how* you made a difference), structure your sentence in the following format:

- Include how you made a difference
- Connect by using the word *by*
- List the action performed (verb ending in—*ing*)

Example

Before

- *Conducted inventory audits of oil rig stockrooms in the Gulf of Mexico*

After

- *Increased efficiency of offshore rig operations <u>by</u> conduct<u>ing</u> inventory audits of oil rig stockrooms in the Gulf of Mexico*

(For your convenience, I underlined the words when *and* by *and letters—*ing *in the examples above. However, do not underline these words on your resume.)*

Always Use Bullets

In general, each item pertaining to your job description should be in bullet format. This will allow the recruiter to read your resume faster. If you write what you did in a paragraph form instead of a bullet form, the recruiter will most likely not read everything you included in the resume. With as many talented candidates submitting resumes on a daily basis, recruiters spend less than thirty seconds, on average, reading each. To be effective, *always* use bullets.

Should I End Each Bullet with a Period?

Please note that the frameworks I provided earlier have phrases rather than sentences. As a result, a period is not necessary at the end of each phrase.

Each Bullet Should Be Kept to One or Two Lines

Again, the fewer words you can use to describe what you did, what you learned, and skills gained, or how you made a difference, the better. If you have to use two lines of resume space for a particular bullet, go ahead. However, one line per bullet is preferred. Three or more lines for a particular bullet is too much and will most likely not be read.

Each Role Should Have at Least Three Bullets

How much work experience you have per position held will dictate how many bullets you include for each role. However, *at minimum*, there should be three bullets *per role* listed on the resume. My general rule for college students or recent graduates is to keep their resume one-page long. Take this into consideration as you write your bullets for each position held.

Each Bullet Should Begin with a Verb

Every bullet should start with a verb because it will show you accomplished something from the start. For example, take a look at the two bullets below. *(For your convenience, I have underlined the verb. However, do not underline the verb on your resume.)*

- *Data collection for the industrial engineer*
- *Collected data for the industrial engineer*

The second bullet sounds stronger because it shows action. Take a look at this example:

- *Training manual was developed for new process*
- *Developed a training manual for a new process*

Again, the second bullet sounds stronger because it shows action from the start.

As a reminder, since you will always be starting with a verb, you never need to start the bullet with a pronoun such as *I*. For example, take a look at the two bullets below for a job you are currently doing. The first is incorrect because it does not start with a verb, and it includes the pronoun *I*.

- *I collected data for the Industrial Engineer*
- *Collected data for the Industrial Engineer*

Take a look at this other example:

- *I developed training manuals for new processes*
- *Developed training manuals for new processes*

Again, the second bullet is the correct one because it starts with a verb and eliminates the pronoun *I*.

Use the Correct Tense

Ensure that activities that have taken place in the past are in past simple tense and those that you are still performing are in present simple tense. Don't get scared if you have no idea what that means! Below are examples of these tenses to help you:

Activities you are involved in right now or in your current role (present simple tense) are the following:

- *demonstrate*
- *deploy*
- *evaluate*
- *arrange*
- *assemble*

Activities you were involved with in the past or in past roles (past simple tense) are the following:

- *demonstrated*
- *deployed*
- *evaluated*
- *arranged*
- *assembled*

For example, the following bullet would NOT be appropriate for a position that took place in the past because the tense indicates an action that is still being performed by you:

- *Evaluate weekly advertising reports*

The verb *evaluate* should be written in past simple tense since this activity took place in the past. Please see below for the correct tense:

- *Evaluated weekly advertising reports*

Can I Use the Same Verb for Every Bullet?

Make sure to start each bullet with a different verb. Using the same verb back-to-back for different bullets will not flow as well, so be as diverse as possible with the verbs you choose to begin your bullets.

To assist you, below is a list of verbs you can use, but feel free to use any verb you may not find on this list, and please take into consideration the grammar rules. *(Please note that all the verbs below are in past simple tense.)*

- accomplished
- achieved
- acquired
- administered
- aided
- analyzed
- answered
- arranged
- assembled
- coordinated
- created
- cut
- decreased
- demonstrated
- deployed
- designated
- designed
- determined
- developed
- diminished
- gained
- gathered
- gave
- generated
- governed

- assisted
- attained
- averted
- budgeted
- calculated
- categorized
- changed
- classified
- coached
- directed
- discussed
- displayed
- edited
- educated
- eliminated
- encouraged
- enforced
- ensured
- eradicated
- established
- minimized
- motivated
- negotiated
- obtained
- operated

- collected
- communicated
- completed
- computed
- conducted
- confirmed
- constructed
- consulted
- controlled
- estimated
- evaluated
- examined
- exchanged
- exhibited
- explored
- facilitated
- forecasted
- formed
- formulated
- fulfilled
- retained
- revealed
- reviewed
- scheduled
- served

- granted
- guaranteed
- guided
- handled
- helped
- implemented
- improved
- induced
- informed
- initiated
- inspired
- installed
- instructed
- investigated
- launched
- lessened
- made
- maintained
- managed
- manufactured
- mastered
- ordered
- organized
- originated
- oversaw
- performed
- planned
- predicted
- prepared
- presented
- prevented
- produced
- programmed
- proofread
- provided
- purchased
- reached
- realized
- reduced
- removed
- researched
- responded
- set up
- showed
- shrank
- sorted
- stimulated
- studied
- supervised
- supplied
- supported
- sustained
- taught
- trained
- tutored
- upheld
- used
- worked
- wrote

Avoid Acronyms

It is easy to get used to company-specific terms and acronyms. However, avoid using acronyms in your resume because most recruiters will not know what they stand for, making your bullets lose value. Instead, spell out the term making up the acronym. For example, let's say that *NAO* is a term used frequently at a specific company and one you wish to include in your resume. Recruiters from different companies are not going to know that *NAO* stands for North American Operations, so you should spell it out as such in the resume.

Quantify When Possible

Quantifying or using numbers to describe your work-related results gives the recruiter a better idea of the magnitude of your accomplishments. You do not need to quantify the contents of every bullet, but do so if possible. Table 6.6 contains a short list of the many items that can be quantified.

Table 6.6. Examples of quantifiable objects.

Items That Are Quantifiable	Example
Revenue generation	$20,000 revenue generated
Percentage improvement	56% customer satisfaction improvement
Percentage reduction	20% employee turnover reduction
Time savings	31% cycle time reduction
Cost savings	$300,000 savings produced

To provide further clarity, take a look at the examples below. *(I have underlined the words that have been quantified. However, do not underline them on your resume):*

Example 1

- *Reduced inventory levels in the factory*
- *Reduced inventory levels in the factory by 20%*

As you can see, the second bullet is stronger because it incorporates the degree to which the level of inventory was reduced (20%).

Example 2

- *Created a model for the finance department*
- *Increased revenue by 5% by creating a model for the finance department*

Again, the second bullet is stronger because it shows by how much the revenue was increased (5%). Continue reviewing the examples below so you can see the effect of quantifying. The second bullet in each example below paints a better picture:

Example 3

- *Shortened cycle time in a key hospital process*
- *Produced annual savings of $50K by shortening the cycle time of a key hospital process by 2 days*

Example 4

- *Managed budget and coordination of vendors*
- *Managed $250K budget and coordination of 20+ vendors*

Example 5

- *Increased revenue through creative sales techniques and positive employee coaching*
- *Increased revenue by 10% through creative sales techniques and positive employee coaching*

Example 6

- *Created and currently update document management systems using XYZ application*
- *Created and currently update document management systems for 350+ project records using XYZ application*

Example 7

- *Developed a marketing campaign*
- *Increased quarterly revenue by 30% by developing an efficient marketing campaign*

Example 8

- *Provided care for cancer patients*
- *Provided care for <u>50+</u> cancer patients*

I think you are starting to see how quantifying the bullets can be used to your advantage. In this case, the second bullet painted a better picture every time. As a reminder, you do not need to quantify every single bullet but doing so when possible is beneficial.

What Do I Do If I Do Not Know or Remember How Much Money My Project or Efforts Saved or Produced?

This is a common question. If you are still working at the same company where you completed the project in question, ask your manager for assistance in quantifying the results of your efforts. Depending on the situation, your manager may also direct you to speak with someone in the finance department who might be able to provide you with those numbers. However, this is at your discretion depending on how comfortable you feel asking your supervisor for help.

You Do Not Need to Describe Everything You Have Done in a Particular Job

It is not necessary to list everything you have done in a past position but rather include those experiences and skills gained that *the recruiter is looking for to match up with those in the job posting.* For example, if one of the job requirements indicates that great customer service is required and you worked in a place where you interacted with customers, then list this experience in your resume. For example:

- *Demonstrated <u>strong customer service</u> when performing financial transactions*

If a job posting requires the ability to work with different departments, you could write:

- *<u>Worked with cross-functional groups</u> when assisting the manager to develop a marketing plan*

Another requirement of a different job may be that the ideal candidate has strong leadership skills. A potential bullet in this case may be:

- *Used <u>strong leadership skills</u> when developing and executing an effective public relations plan for a client*

To summarize, always let the job posting requirements guide you in crafting the bullets in your resume. However, in the event you do not have all the required skills, you may list those that could be relevant for the job. Keep in mind that the more skills you have that match the specific job posting, the stronger the chance you will be asked for an interview.

What Do I Do If I Do Not Possess Any of the Requirements in the Job Posting?

Many people apply to jobs that do not fit their skills set and are surprised when they do not get an interview. If you are applying for a job where you do not meet any of the requirements in the job posting, I encourage you to ask yourself why you are applying. With that said, always be honest about the skills you do have and include those in your resume.

The General Resume

Many people I work with are not applying for a specific job, but they just want to have a resume available. It is good to have one because you never know when someone will inform you of a job opportunity or internship that will require your resume in less than twenty-four hours. Additionally, updating it frequently will prevent you from forgetting your accomplishments.

While I was an undergrad at the University of Houston, I was told that a recruiter from Continental Airlines was looking for resumes for a summer internship but needed to make a decision as soon as possible. It was to my advantage that I had a complete resume ready to turn in because I was able to interview shortly after and, eventually, received the internship.

When completing a general resume, you are not going to have a job posting in front of you where you can see the required skills and experiences for a specific role. This is okay as long as you follow the recommendations provided earlier (e.g., describe your job duties from past roles, explain what you learned, skills gained/used, how you made a difference, use verbs, quantify when possible, etc.).

Do I Use the Same Resume for Different Job Applications?

If you are applying for multiple jobs, you may end up having to tweak your general resume a few times depending on what jobs you are applying for. The key here is that you have a separate resume for each job posting, including relevant skills and experiences from your past that are required for each.

For example, if you are applying for three separate internships in three different consumer banks and all involve working in the finance department, then you will most likely apply for all with the same resume. Why? Most likely, the three different job postings will have similar requirements.

However, if you are applying for three separate internships—which require working in the finance department of either a bank, an oil company, or an accounting firm—you may end up having to tweak your general resume three times. These will most likely be similar but altered a little bit to ensure you match the specific skills and experiences from your past with the three different roles.

You Do Not Need to Include Every Job You Have Done in Your Life

Some people have the benefit of having worked for several years. Perhaps you worked while you were in high school and then had other jobs while in college. For people who have adequate past work experience, it is not necessary to mention on the resume everywhere you have worked. The key is to start with the most recent place you have worked or are working (use reverse chronological order), and as mentioned in the previous section, "pull" experiences that support you for the role you are applying for.

Let's say Mary is preparing her resume for a job in a chemical laboratory. Table 6.7 represents her work experience:

Table 6.7. Mary's work experience.

Age	Occupation
16	Waitress at local diner
17	Ticket agent at movie theater
18	Teacher assistant for chemistry class
19	Bank teller

Should she include all the jobs she has performed? The job posting indicates that the ideal candidate should have the ability to work with vendors in addition to ten other requirements. Mary has gained the additional ten by working as a teacher assistant and as a bank teller (her last two jobs). Since she worked closely with all the food and beverage vendors while employed at the movie theater, she should go ahead and list the ticket agent role as well. Now that she has shown all the requirements on the job posting, there is no need to include her first role, the waitress at the local diner.

Your Past Jobs: Brainstorming

To help you gather your thoughts, use the next few pages to list up to three jobs. If you have held more than three in the past, feel free to continue the exercise using a sheet of paper. Fill as much as you can and then transfer the information to your resume.

Job 1

Name of company: _____

Job title: _____

Dates of employment: _____

City and state of employment: _____

What were your job duties?

_____

_____

_____

What did you learn?

_____

_____

_____

What skills did you gain?

_____

_____

_____

How did you make a difference?

_____

_____

_____

Job 2

Name of company: _____

Job title: _____

Dates of employment: _____

City and state of employment: _____

What were your job duties?

_____

_____

_____

What did you learn?

_____

_____

_____

What skills did you gain?

_____

_____

_____

How did you make a difference?

_____

_____

_____

Job 3

Name of company: _____

Job title: _____

Dates of employment: _____

City and state of employment: _____

What were your job duties?

_____

_____

_____

What did you learn?

_____

_____

_____

What skills did you gain?

_____

_____

_____

How did you make a difference?

_____

_____

_____

What Do I Do If I Do Not Have Formal Work Experience?

If you have not worked in the job market before, then leave out the work experience section. The next chapter will teach you how to evaluate skills acquired in other activities.

Chapter 7

Technical and Nontechnical Skills

In this chapter, you will learn how to list both technical and nontechnical skills on your resume.

Technical skills refer to the numerical, scientific, and computer-related competencies and knowledge needed to accomplish specific job tasks. For example, knowledge of Microsoft Excel is useful to engineers, business analysts, and scientists; knowing how to use a stethoscope is crucial for a nurse; and being able to use computer-aided design software is important for a fashion designer.

Nontechnical skills refer to personal and social qualities such as the ability to work well in a team, communicate effectively, display leadership, and learn new information quickly.

Highlight both technical and nontechnical skills in your resume using one of the three different approaches listed below.

Approach 1

Incorporate your technical and nontechnical skills into your job description bullets as mentioned in the work experience section.

(For your convenience, I have underlined the skills in the bullets below. However, do not underline them on your resume. Also, note that some are in the present tense.)

- Exemplified <u>strong leadership</u> when supervising the team in the absence of the store manager
- <u>Paid close attention to detail</u> when processing sales transactions, returns, and orders
- <u>Demonstrated trust and ethical behavior</u> by maintaining attorney-client privilege for all confidential information
- Displayed the <u>ability to use computer-modeling techniques</u> that resulted in efficient and feasible design solutions
- <u>Created forecasts</u> for the communications department by using <u>Access</u> and <u>Excel</u> programs
- Showed the <u>ability to work with others</u> when participating in work sessions with public policy consultants
- Utilized <u>Cisco WebEx</u> to facilitate virtual meetings with senior managers

Approach 2

Create a separate section labeled *Summary of Qualifications* to specify your technical and nontechnical skills.

This approach is typically used whenever you do not have any work experience or if you have more skills than you can fit within the work experience section. This part should come after the education section. Fig. 7-1 is an example of a partial resume using approach 2.

HERBERT BROWN

64903 Oak Meadow Street
Dallas, TX 34579
342.543.3655
Herbert.Brown34@mail.com

OBJECTIVE
Self-motivated and detail-oriented graduate with computing and analytical skills looking for a laboratory technologist position within the pharmaceutical industry

EDUCATION
University of Southern California-Dornsife College of Letters, Arts, and Sciences   **GPA: 3.7**
Bachelor of Science in Chemistry   Minor: Physics   Los Angeles, CA   08/2009-05/2013

SUMMARY OF QUALIFICATIONS
- Expertise in laboratory distribution module software
- Proficiency in MS Word, Excel, and PowerPoint
- Excellent communication and analytical skills
- Ability to analyze and interpret technical reports

WORK EXPERIENCE
ABC Chemicals   06/2013-present   Broussard, Louisiana
Lab Operator
- Ensure compliance with quality standards by performing daily lab inspections
- Pay close attention to detail when preparing lab samples for corporate clients
- Improve product output by performing proactive maintenance of lab equipment
- Develop and maintain data base to accurately record and track defect trends

Figure 7-1. Partial resume using skills approach 2.

Approach 3

Create a specific section for your *technical* skills separate from your nontechnical skills.

This section can be labeled *Technical Skills*. Typically, you should choose approach 3 if you are applying for a position requiring technical knowledge.

If I Have a Specific Section for My Technical Skills, Where Do I Include My Nontechnical Skills?

With approach 3, you can also create a separate section highlighting your nontechnical skills or you can incorporate them into the job description bullets in the work experience section.

The partial resume in fig. 7-2 shows technical skills in a section titled *Technical Skills* and nontechnical skills in a section titled *Personal Strengths*.

CHRISTOPHER S. OWENS

9898 Persephone Hills Road
Montpelier, Vermont 23223
(254) 230-3465
Chistopher.Owens@mail.com

Objective
Accomplished and artistic individual with unique web design and typography skills seeking a full-time position as a graphic designer in the sports industry

Education
American University, College of Arts and Sciences   Washington, DC   GPA: 3.60
Bachelor of Arts in Graphic Design   Minor: French   Tentative 5/14

Technical Skills
- Autodesk AutoCAD
- Adobe Photoshop
- Adobe Illustrator
- Adobe Flash
- Dreamweaver HTML
- Microsoft Word
- Microsoft PowerPoint
- Microsoft Excel

Personal Strengths
- Exceptional written and oral communication and presentation skills
- Detail-oriented and excellent multitasking ability
- Excellent ability to maneuver through intricate organizational structures
- Strong ethical standards, reliability, and accountability

Work Experience
HJKE&R, Graphic Design Intern   Miami, Florida   January 2013-May 2013
- Explored different design typologies based on extensive survey data
- Gained experience working with cross-functional teams when developing new product marketing design
- Exemplified strong creativity when developing effective brochures, application kits, and flyers for clients

Figure 7-2. Partial resume using skills approach 3.

Fig. 7-3 contains an example of a partial resume using approach 3, incorporating the technical skills in a specific section on the resume while the nontechnical skills are included within the job description bullets. *(For your convenience, I have underlined the nontechnical skills. However, do not underline the skills on your resume.)*

Nicole R. Smith

12334 Long Shadow Street
New Orleans, Louisiana
934-265-5616
nicole.r.smith@mail.com

Objective

Talented and proactive undergraduate with strong business acumen and technical aptitude seeking a career in operations management in the agriculture industry

Education

California State University—Chico College of Agriculture   Chico, California
Bachelor of Science in Agricultural Business   **GPA:** 3.8   Expected May 2014

Technical Skills

- Proficient in Microsoft Office systems: Access, Excel, Outlook, PowerPoint, and Word
- Proficient in agricultural systems: WinPig, ABECAS, AGRIS V9, ExtendAg, AgManager Package 4, AgCheck Accounting, PeachTree Accounting, and AgWorks

Employment

Labs XYZ Inc.
Operations Supervisor Intern   Phoenix, Arizona   June 2013-present
- Manage and maintain proper lab inventory levels through careful attention to detail
- Demonstrate responsibility when updating daily records and generating monthly reports for management
- Exemplify strong customer focus when working with suppliers and other business partners
- Cared for livestock when administering preventive care

Figure 7-3. Partial resume using skills approach 3.

What Are Common Nontechnical Skills and Qualities Employers Look For?

Below are some common nontechnical skills and qualities employers look for in potential job candidates. Feel free to incorporate some of these in your resume if you possess them. Please note that those listed below are only a sample of the many skills and qualities employers look for. Make sure to review the ones required in the job postings.

- Ability to influence
- Ability to lead
- Ability to motivate others
- Ability to prioritize
- Ability to teach/coach
- Accountable
- Adjusts well to change
- Analytical
- Approachable
- Comfortable around different levels of the organization
- Confident
- Creative
- Deals well with ambiguity
- Decisive
- Demonstrate integrity/ethics
- Drive for results
- Effective listener
- Evaluate risks
- Excellent presentation skills
- Excellent time management
- Flexible
- Focus on safety
- Great at tactical execution
- Great communication skills
- Great interpersonal skills
- Great judgment
- Innovative
- Organized
- Promotes teamwork
- Quality-focused
- Rapid learner
- Reliable
- Self-motivated
- Set realistic goals
- Strategic thinker
- Strong business acumen
- Strong customer focus
- Strong problem solver
- Strong technical aptitude
- Take initiative

The next chapter will show you the proper placement of awards and personal achievements in your resume.

Chapter 8

Awards, Achievements, and Honors

Including awards, achievements, and/or honors in the resume will exhibit your recognized strengths and make your resume more appealing. You can choose one of two different approaches to help you describe your awards, achievements, and honors.

Approach 1

Create a section in your resume specifically for your awards, achievements, and honors.

This segment can go anywhere after the education section. Below are different names you can use to label this section:

- Awards
- Honors
- Achievements
- Recognitions
- Accolades
- Combination of the names listed above (e.g., Awards and Honors)

Fig. 8-1 shows an example of a partial resume with an awards section that highlights achievements and recognition.

SOPHIA A. CANNON

2691 Saint Charles Avenue
Boston, MA 44009

(985) 372-8529
sofia.cannon@mail.com

OBJECTIVE

Energetic and driven individual with exceptional persuasion and listening skills seeking a sales opportunity in the computer hardware industry

EDUCATION

Boston University, School of Management   Boston, MA   Expected May 2013
Bachelor of Science in Business Administration   **GPA:** 4.0

SUMMARY OF QUALIFICATIONS

- Outstanding customer service and sales techniques
- Supportive and motivating team member
- Exceptional organizational skills for multiple task management and project completion
- Detail-oriented and excellent communication skills
- Proficient in QuickBooks 2007-2009, Quicken 2008, and Microsoft Office 2007

AWARDS

Platinum Award for Top Summer Intern, southeast region, 2012   Westcott Computers Inc.
Most Dedicated Volunteer of the Year, 2011   Hearts for the Homeless
National Society of Business Scholars inductee, 2011   Boston University

WORK EXPERIENCE

Westcott Computer Company
Sales intern   Boston, MA   *June 2012-August 2012*
- Demonstrated strong financial acumen when forecasting daily sales and related costs
- Increased revenue of southeast region by 14% by negotiating computer sales contracts
- Utilized excellent communication skills when assisting clients in acquiring Westcott products
- Gained strong knowledge of sales policies and procedures when assisting sales manager
- Provided excellent customer service to clients in southeast region by creating work orders

COMMUNITY SERVICE

- Hearts for the Homeless, 2011
- Recycling Friends of America, 2012

Figure 8-1. Partial resume with an awards section.

Approach 2

Incorporate awards in other sections of the resume as applicable.

Fig. 8-2 represents the same partial resume shown earlier but with awards highlighted in the education, work experience, and community service sections. (*We will discuss the community service section in more detail in an upcoming chapter. For your convenience, I have italicized and set in boldface the awards. However, do not italicize or set in boldface the actual awards on your resume.*)

SOPHIA A. CANNON

2691 Saint Charles Avenue
Boston, MA 44009

(985) 372-8529
sofia.cannon@mail.com

OBJECTIVE

Energetic and driven individual with exceptional persuasion and listening skills seeking a sales opportunity in the computer hardware industry

EDUCATION

Boston University, School of Management   Boston, MA   Expected May 2013
Bachelor of Science in Business Administration   **GPA:** 4.0
National Society of Business Scholars inductee, 2011

SUMMARY OF QUALIFICATIONS

- Outstanding customer service and sales techniques
- Supportive and motivating team member
- Exceptional organizational skills for multiple task management and project completion
- Detail-oriented and excellent communication skills
- Proficient in QuickBooks 2007-2009, Quicken 2008, and Microsoft Office 2007

WORK EXPERIENCE

Westcott Computers Inc.
Sales intern   *Boston, MA*   *June 2012-August 2012*
- Demonstrated strong financial acumen when forecasting daily sales and related costs
- Increased revenue of southeast region by 14% by negotiating computer sales contracts
- ***Won Platinum Award for being the top summer intern of the southeast region***
- Utilized excellent communication skills when assisting clients in acquiring Westcott products
- Gained strong knowledge of sales policies and procedures when assisting sales manager
- Provided excellent customer service to clients in southeast region when creating work orders

COMMUNITY SERVICE

- Hearts for the Homeless, ***Most Dedicated Volunteer of the Year, 2011***
- Recycling Friends of America, 2012

Figure 8-2. Partial resume with awards incorporated in other sections.

What Types of Awards, Achievements, and/or Honors Can I Include in the Resume?

Please note that while it is advantageous to list some awards in the resume, others should never be included. For example, Sumit Krishnamurthy is a sophomore economics major applying for an internship or job in the field of economics. In the past three years, he had the following achievements:

1. *Inducted into a freshman honor society for making good grades*
2. *Received first place at a national piano competition during sophomore year*
3. *Won a jalapeño eating contest during freshman year*
4. *Received the intramural soccer team* Most Dedicated Member of the Month *award*
5. *Received straight As during senior year of high school*
6. *Won a beer-chugging competition at a fraternity party*

Which of these awards are acceptable to list on the resume? Let's discuss each in more detail.

Award 1: *Inducted into a freshman honor society for making good grades.* Most individuals would agree that listing this award would be important because it shows that Sumit worked hard to make good grades and therefore understands economics well.

General rule 1

Companies want to hire individuals who are intelligent and will assess intelligence and future performance partly by your grades. Any award received while in college that highlights your academic performance should be listed on the resume.

Award 2: *Received first place at a national piano competition during sophomore year.* This award is not related to economics but is impressive. I would recommend that Sumit include it, if and only if, he still has room on his resume. Companies not only want to hire individuals who are smart but also those who have other diverse talents and desirable skills. Winning a national piano competition shows drive, dedication, and perseverance—skills that companies value.

Now, if Sumit has three other awards that are related to an accomplishment on the piano, I would suggest to him not to list all three piano awards because we do not want the recruiter to think that his strongest talent is piano and not economics.

General rule 2

Awards, honors, or recognitions that highlight your drive, dedication, and perseverance can be listed on the resume as long as they enhance your professional image.

Award 3: *Won a jalapeño eating contest during freshman year.* I am sure most of you agree that Sumit should not list the third award of winning a jalapeño eating contest because it may make him look juvenile and unprofessional; however, one can argue that it also highlights his fun personality, indicating to a recruiter that he is someone whom his coworkers would love to have around in the office, someone who likes competition, and is down-to-earth. In this situation, my advice is as follows:

General rule 3

If you have sufficient content in the resume to show that you are professional, intelligent, and action-driven, *and* you are *not* submitting your resume to a conservative company, it is okay to list a fun personality award because it shows you have an upbeat personality. However, if there is not a good balance between professionalism, good grades, and drive on the resume and you are submitting your resume to a conservative company, then do *not* list it.

Award 4: *Received Most Dedicated Member of the Month award on an intramural soccer team.* Although this award is not economics-related, it shows that Sumit excelled in a team activity. His dedication to the soccer team equates with being a strong team player for the company. I would include this award on the resume.

General rule 4

Companies want to hire individuals who can work well in a team environment; they evaluate team dynamics partly by your involvement in team activities outside of the classroom. Any award received while in college that highlights you as a team player should be listed on the resume.

Award 5: *Received straight As during senior year of high school.* A lot of people may immediately say that Sumit should list this recognition on the resume because it shows that he is intelligent. However, I would hesitate to include this one because a sophomore applying for an internship needs to show that he or she is making good grades while in college, not two years ago while in high school. While making straight As in high school is commendable, current grades in college will always tell a better story to the recruiters.

General rule 5

You do not need to list your high school GPA, high school class rank, high school grades, or awards won before college on the resume.*

*The exception to this rule is if you have only been in college for less than one semester and are applying for an internship and do not have a lot of awards or even a college GPA yet to put on the resume. In this case, you can include a few accolades from high school as long as they are relevant based on our discussion thus far.

Award 6: *Won beer-chugging competition at a fraternity party.* Sumit should never put this award on his resume, especially since he, like many undergrads, may not be legally old enough to drink beer. And even if he was, he is not demonstrating any specific skill that a company may be looking for.

General rule 6

Nothing related to the use of alcohol and drugs should ever be included on the resume.

I hope that Sumit's examples provided you with a good idea of which awards are acceptable in the awards section. The next chapter will show you how you can incorporate leadership skills and extracurricular activities in your resume.

Chapter 9

Extracurricular Activities and Leadership Roles

Many companies not only seek students who perform well academically but also those who are involved in extracurricular activities and leadership roles. These experiences show the employer that you have interacted with other students to accomplish team goals and acquired a variety of skills in the process, which can be directly transferrable to the workplace.

Therefore, you should list your extracurricular activities and leadership roles on the resume. Below are a few names you can choose to label this specific section:

- Leadership Roles
- Extracurricular Activities
- Organizational Involvement
- Club Involvement
- Combination of the above terms (e.g., Leadership Roles and Club Involvement)

This section can be listed anywhere, but I would recommend for it to be placed after the work experience. The extracurricular activities section contains the following components:

- Name of organization or club
- Leadership role held (if any)
- Time held in leadership role and/or club overall

Table 9-1 shows different ways to structure your organizational involvement in the resume.

Table 9-1. How to indicate leadership on your resume.

Format	Example	
Role and name of club followed by month and year	President, XYZ fraternity	August 2012-present
	Treasurer, university soccer team	January 2012-June 2012
Name of club and role followed by month and year	XYZ fraternity, president	August 2012-present
	University soccer team, treasurer	January 2012-June 2012
Role and name of club followed by length of time served	President, XYZ fraternity	one year
	Treasurer, university soccer team	one year
Name of club and role followed by length of time served	XYZ fraternity, president	six months
	University soccer team, treasurer	six months

Fig. 9-1 presents a resume that contains a student's leadership roles in a section titled *Organizational Involvement and Leadership Roles.*

LAWRENCE BENICIO MARTINEZ

5620 Glenloaf Drive
Sugarland, TX 77391

713.339.4949
LBMartinez@yahoo.com

OBJECTIVE: Dedicated and well-organized individual with excellent leadership and technical skills seeking a computer engineering role within the information technology industry

EDUCATION
University of Houston, Cullen College of Engineering   Houston, TX   **GPA: 3.86**
Bachelor of Science in Computer Engineering   Minor: Math   Expected May 2013

WORK EXPERIENCE
Computer World Inc.   Plano, TX   May 2012-August 2012
Computer Engineering Intern
- Reduced data collection time by 15% by introducing new online system for storing data
- Improved quality of testing by introducing two new procedures for performing testing
- Gained valuable experience in writing scripts when assisting teams in planning project's testing phase

Chips and Dip Inc.   El Paso, TX   June 2011-September 2011
Computer Engineering Intern
- Acquired working knowledge of customer network maintenance when shadowing team
- Lessened catalogue content update time by designing code to automate vendor changes
- Exemplified strong communication skills when presenting to executive leadership team

ACADEMIC AWARDS, ACHIEVEMENTS, AND HONORS
- Most Outstanding Computer Engineering Junior, 2013
- 2011 Brother of the Year, Beta Beta Beta International Fraternity Inc.
- Induction into Sigma Sigma Sigma Computer Engineering National Honor Society, 2009

TECHNICAL SKILLS
Pascal, Fortran, Mathcad, Microsoft Office, Matlab, Control System, Simulation, Linux, Agile

ORGANIZATIONAL INVOLVEMENT AND LEADERSHIP ROLES
- President (one year)   Delta Delta National Leadership Honor Society
- President (two years)   Hispanic Student Association
- Vice President (one year)   Helping Hand (community service-related club)
- Vice President (six months)   Sigma Sigma Sigma National Honor Society
- Membership Director (one year)   Institute of Computer Engineering Students
- District Officer (one year)   Beta Beta Beta International Fraternity Inc.
- Principal Violinist (three years)   University of Houston symphony orchestra
- Treasurer (one year)   University of Houston golf team

Figure 9-1. Resume with numerous leadership roles highlighted.

What Qualifies as a Leadership Role?

Any regular participation in a college organization, club, community initiative, religious group, sports team, musical group, fraternity or sorority, professional society, and project or event can be listed on the resume as a leadership role.

Below are some good examples of common leadership roles in organizations/groups:

- President
- Vice President
- Treasurer
- Historian
- Secretary
- Public Relations chair
- Parliamentarian
- Community Service chair
- Recruitment director
- Social director
- Student/faculty liaison
- Editor-in-chief
- Team captain
- Quarterback
- Principal musician
- Drum Major
- Event chairman
- Chaplain

What Do I Do If I Have Never Held a Leadership Role?

This section should be left out if you have never held a leadership role or led an activity. However, I would strongly recommend that you run for an officer or leadership position to get a better idea of what it takes to motivate other members of your group, what types of organizational skills are needed to run a club successfully, and how to manage your time between school (or work) and club responsibilities. Having leadership roles on your resume will improve your chances of being interviewed. If you are involved in a club but you are not an officer, you can indicate that you are an active member as long as it is true.

The next section will discuss how to list knowledge of multiple languages on your resume.

© 2005 Ted Goff

"How would you describe
my leadership?
Great, greater or greatest?"

Chapter 10

Languages Spoken

If you speak or have working knowledge of more than one language, recruiters strongly encourage you to include this on your resume. You can mention this in the skills section, or you can include your language proficiencies in a separate section titled *Languages*.

Table 10-1 represents the different formats wherein you can include *all* the languages you speak.

Table 10-1. Language entry format examples.

Format	Example
Language and proficiency	English (fluent) or English (fluent), Spanish (advanced)
Language and years studied	Spanish (four years) or Spanish (four years), German (three years)
Language with written and oral skills specified	English (fluent in written and oral communication) or English (fluent in written and oral communication), Spanish (advanced in written and oral communication)

Also, when you speak a language, you may have different levels of proficiency, both spoken and written. These should also be specified on the resume. For your convenience, table 10-2 describes different levels of language proficiency.

Table 10-2. Different levels of language proficiency.

Skill Level	Description
Basic or beginner	• You have had one or two years of classes in a particular language. • You can express simple sentences but do not understand native speakers.
Intermediate or conversational	• You have had two or more years of classes in a particular language. • You can form simple sentences. • You are able to write and speak with limited vocabulary. • Native speakers understand you even though you might make errors. • You can understand native speakers about 25 percent of the time.
Advanced	• You have had three or more years of classes in a particular language. • You are able to write and speak in the foreign language with decent vocabulary and grammar. • Native speakers of the language can understand you even though you might make errors. • You can understand native speakers about 50 percent or more of the time.
Fluent	• You have had more than four years of classes in a particular language. • You are able to write and speak in a particular language with little mistakes. • Native speakers of the language have little trouble understanding you. • You have little trouble understanding native speakers. • You are able to engage in more complex discussions with native speakers.

Fig. 10-1 is an example of a resume with the languages included in the skills section.

PREETHA A. SANCHEZ

301 West Elm Road
Oakland, CA 44356
Preetha.Sanchez@mail.com
445-367-6678

OBJECTIVE
Sharp and confident student with design and marketing skills seeking a full time position in print and digital journalism within the international affairs broadcasting industry

EDUCATION
University of Southern California, Annenberg School for Communication and Journalism
Bachelor of Arts in Print and Digital Journalism   Los Angeles, CA   Tentative: 12/14

SKILLS
Proficient in Microsoft Office Systems: Access, Excel, Outlook, PowerPoint, and Word
Languages: English (fluent), standard Hindi (fluent), Spanish (advanced), Japanese (three years)

EXPERIENCE
June 2013-August 2013   **BCS Communication Group Inc.**   Woodland Hills, CA
Journalism Intern
  - Gained exposure to executive leadership team when performing daily administrative tasks for the company's CEO/president
  - Reviewed and responded to CEO's correspondence and provided effective notes and status updates
  - Showed strong planning skills when coordinating four media/promotional tours and three regional programs and events
  - Exemplified effective administration skills when scheduling weekly meetings with clients and preparing strategic meeting agendas
  - Demonstrated strong time management and multitasking skills when distributing news releases for time-sensitive breaking news while balancing daily routines and initiatives

June 2012-August 2012   **Coastal Products Limited**   San Francisco, CA
Advertising/Marketing Intern
  - Showcased superior design skills when creating attractive page layouts for monthly publications
  - Edited English documents daily and translated them to Spanish for Latin American clients
  - Used adequate diplomacy when representing the company at the annual Coastal Technology Conference

Figure 10-1. Resume with languages included in skills section.

Fig. 10-2 is an example of an almost identical resume with the languages included in a separate languages section.

PREETHA A. SANCHEZ

301 West Elm Road
Oakland, CA 44356

Preetha.Sanchez@mail.com
445-367-6678

OBJECTIVE
Sharp and confident student with design and marketing skills seeking a full-time position in print and digital journalism within the international affairs broadcasting industry

EDUCATION
University of Southern California,   Los Angeles, CA
Annenberg School for Communication and Journalism
Bachelor of Arts in Print and Digital Journalism   Tentative 12/14

SKILLS
Proficient in Microsoft Office Systems: Access, Excel, Outlook, PowerPoint, and Word

EXPERIENCE
June 2013-August 2013   **BCS Communication Group Inc.**   Woodland Hills, CA
Journalism intern
- Gained exposure to executive leadership team when performing daily administrative tasks for the company's CEO/president
- Showed strong planning skills when coordinating four media/promotional tours and three regional programs and events
- Exemplified effective administration skills when scheduling weekly meetings with clients and preparing strategic meeting agendas

June 2012-August 2012   **Coastal Products Limited**   San Francisco, CA
Advertising/marketing intern
- Showcased superior design skills when creating attractive page layouts for monthly publications
- Edited English documents daily and translated them to Spanish for Latin American clients
- Used adequate diplomacy when representing the company at the annual Coastal Technology Conference

LANGUAGES
English (fluent), standard Hindi (fluent), Spanish (advanced), Japanese (three years)

Figure 10-2. Resume with a languages section.

What Do I Do If I Do Not Remember Much of the Language I May Have Studied?

If you took German classes, for example, for three years but have forgotten everything you have learned, then you do not have working knowledge of German and should not include it in the resume. The last thing you want is to be assigned a task where you have to use your German skills and not be able to execute it.

This completes the required sections of the resume. The next few chapters will discuss optional sections to include if space permits.

"You speak Gobbledygook!
Excellent!"

Chapter 11

Optional Section: Community Service

Some college students have the opportunity to participate in community service events, perhaps as members of a student organization or in extracurricular activities. Although not required, these volunteer opportunities may have allowed you to gain leadership skills, which can be transferrable to the workplace. Therefore, it is okay to list them on the resume.

Community service events can be included in the extracurricular activities section or you can create a separate section specifically for community service. If you choose to include one, place it somewhere after the work experience segment and label it in one of the following ways:

- Community Involvement
- Community Service
- Community Service Events
- Philanthropic Efforts

How Many Community Service Events Can I Include in My Resume?

Please keep in mind that you do not want to fill the entire resume with community service events you have participated in. Including anywhere between three to five events is acceptable.

If you have space available in your resume, then you can add more, but your employer will be looking closer at the previous sections (education, work experience, skills, honors, etc.), so it is important that you try to fill as much as possible within these sections before you begin to add the community service events.

What Components Make Up the Community Service Section?

For the community service section, at minimum, you should write the name of the community service agency where you served as a volunteer. For example, the following represents community service agencies where I have volunteered:

- *American Red Cross*
- *Susan G. Komen Race for the Cure*
- *Third Ward House Restoration Project*
- *Neighborhood Impact*

If you have enough room on the resume, you can also mention in a few words how you made a difference for the organization (start with a verb when describing your contributions). See below:

- *American Red Cross—led three marketing campaigns*
- *Susan G. Komen Race for the Cure—raised $5.6K*
- *Third Ward House Restoration Project—trained ten volunteers*
- *Neighborhood Impact—removed graffiti from one community building wall*

OR

- *Led three marketing campaigns for the American Red Cross*
- *Raised $5.6K for Susan G. Komen Race for the Cure*
- *Trained ten volunteers for the Third Ward House Restoration Project*

- *Removed graffiti from a wall in one community building through Neighborhood Impact*

If you want to show that you were involved extensively with a particular philanthropy or nonprofit organization, you can also specify the time period or the number of hours that you worked. See below:

- *American Red Cross—led three marketing campaigns (40 hours)*
- *Susan G. Komen Race for the Cure, raised $5.6K (March 2012-March 2013)*
- *Third Ward House Restoration Project, trained ten volunteers—20 hours*
- *Neighborhood Impact, removed graffiti from one community building—December 2011*

Fig. 11-1 contains a partial resume with a separate community service section.

SANFORD JENKINS

4578 Yellow Bud Street
Las Vegas, NV 78759

957-326-3956
sanford.jenkins@mail.com

Objective
Collaborative and influential individual with positive and team-oriented personality pursuing an opportunity in higher education administration

Education
University of Nevada-Las Vegas, College of Liberal Arts   Las Vegas, NV
Bachelor of Arts in Political Science, Minor: English
Expected May 2015   **GPA:** 3.81

Technical Skills
Microsoft Word, Excel, PowerPoint, Access, Outlook, Visio, Mac OS X

Work Experience
Nevada Bank
Teller   *Las Vegas, NV*   *August 2011-July 2013*
- Demonstrated strong oral communication skills when assisting customers with everyday banking needs
- Assisted team members during peak hours to promote a cohesive team environment and reduce wait times by 50%
- Provided exceptional customer service when operating cash drawer for commercial window
- Resolved customer complaints by using active listening skills and reacting quickly

Community Involvement
- Raised $1,305 as team captain for Women's Society and $2,385 as team captain for Asthma Society of Nevada, 2014
- Led a political science workshop for youth during college day, 2012 and 2013
- Volunteered for Libraries of Kids, Nevada Food Bank, and Las Vegas Community Center, 2013

Figure 11-1. Partial resume with community service section.

In the next chapter, you'll learn how to add your international travels on your resume.

Chapter 12

Optional Section: International Travel

Most people who visit a foreign country typically experience intellectual and personal growth by interacting with the locals and being exposed to the country's culture, language, geography, architecture, food, and history. Given that we are connected to a global economy, companies seek students who can think globally. The best way to expose you to international ideas is by actually visiting different countries. Therefore, if you have some international travel experience, another optional section you can place in the resume is international travel.

This section can go anywhere on the resume, but I would recommend placing it somewhere after the work experience section. It can be labeled as follows:

- International Travel
- Global Travel
- Travel
- Countries Visited

Below are a few tips to add information to the resume's international travel section:

- List countries you have visited outside of the United States for study, leisure, and/or work.
- Do not enter the dates you traveled.

Fig. 12-1 is a resume with an international travel section for a student who is working while going to school.

SUSAN MARIE CHEN

301 West Elm Road
Charlotte, NC 44356

Susan.Chen12@mail.com
445-367-6678

OBJECTIVE
Cosmopolitan and competent student with excellent oral and written communication skills seeking a public relations internship in the telecommunication industry

EDUCATION
University of Georgia, Franklin College of Arts and Science   Athens, GA   **GPA:** 3.6
Bachelor of Arts in Communication Studies,   Minor: Theater   Expected December 2014

SKILLS
- Proficient in Microsoft Office Systems: Access, Excel, Outlook, PowerPoint, and Word
- Ability to write press releases and promotional materials
- Skillful in developing computer graphics techniques for media productions

WORK EXPERIENCE
August 2012-present   **Ventura Inc.**   **Charleston, SC**
Executive assistant
- Perform all administrative tasks such as preparing executive presentations, scheduling travel arrangements, and ordering office supplies
- Introduced the office recycling program to contribute to Ventura's culture of sustainability—site was recognized as green office of the week
- Organize team-spirit activities, such as monthly potlucks, as the chair of the spirit committee
- Maintain company organized by conducting expense reimbursement duties for the site

AWARDS
- Recipient of the Brilliance Award at the Freshman Fundraising Competition ($23K)
- Inducted into the Communications Honor Society, 2012
- Winner of the Media Production Program Member of the Year award, 2011

LEADERSHIP ROLES
- Treasurer   Communications Society of America   January 2013-present
- Team captain   Intramural basketball   February 2012-January 2013
- Active member Communities for Georgia   March 2011-December 2011

INTERNATIONAL TRAVEL

• Mexico	• Spain	• Australia
• Costa Rica	• The Netherlands	• New Zealand
• Panama	• Egypt	• Singapore
• Venezuela	• Thailand	• Vietnam
• France	• China	• Russia

Figure 12-1. Resume with international travel section.

The next chapter will discuss how you can include projects in the resume.

Chapter 13

Optional Section: Special Projects

While in school, many students have the opportunity to work on challenging projects, which provide useful knowledge they can use in their desired jobs. For example, in one of my engineering undergraduate classes, four students and I designed and constructed several unique vibration dampers (devices used to reduce vibrations). This gave us the opportunity to utilize several project management tools and refine our analytical skills.

Another great experience in one of my upper-level engineering classes was when I was required to evaluate a specific process of a major corporation and provide ergonomic improvement recommendations. This gave me important insight into the design of company workstations to improve safety.

Another stimulating opportunity involved collecting data for an industrial engineer to serve as input into a special model he was creating. I learned innovative methods to create a model that would help reduce customers' wait times.

If you had the opportunity to complete one or more special projects that taught you professional skills a recruiter is looking for, you can list them in a separate section anywhere after the education section labeled as follows:

- Special Projects
- Class Projects
- University-Sponsored Projects
- College-Sponsored Projects

When listing a special project, keep each entry within two lines and provide the following:

- Name of project
- Name of class
- Description of what you did, what you learned, skills you gained, or how you made a difference. Use the same rules specified in the work experience segment.

Fig. 13-1 provides an example of a resume with a special projects section.

RUBEN BRYAN ARMSTRONG

4800 Long Meadow Street   704-345-6789
Charlotte, NC 23456   Ruben.Armstrong@mail.com

Career Objective
Dynamic and innovative student with exceptional analytical and modeling skills searching for an industrial engineering internship within the airline industry

Education
The University of Houston-Cullen College of Engineering   Houston, TX   **GPA:** 3.75
Bachelor of Science in Industrial Engineering   Minor: Business   Expected May 2014

Special Projects
- *XYZ Company Workstation Ergonomic Improvements*—(class: Human Factors)—provided ergonomic improvement recommendations by performing analysis on workstations
- *Traffic Light Vibration Reduction*—(class: Design IV)—decreased traffic light post vibrations by designing and constructing four dampers
- *Rainbow Airlines Ticket Counter Optimization*—(class: Simulation)—reduced customers' wait times by collecting data on ticket counter check-in process

Work Experience
June 2013-August 2013   HRS&T Steel Manufacturing LLC   Alvin, Texas
Industrial Engineering Intern
- Reduced overall scrap by 23% by performing time study on key manufacturing processes
- Gained relevant knowledge on safety methodologies when assisting the operations manager
- Obtained vital presentation skills when delivering project results to the plant's director
- Created a scorecard for evaluating productivity and quality goals

Awards
- Cullen College of Engineering Design Competition, Second Place winner   2013
- La Hacienda Twenty-fifth Anniversary Scholarship recipient   2013
- Officer of the Year, Student Government   2012

Leadership Roles and Organizational Involvement
- President—Alpha Industrial Engineering Honor Society   May 2013-present
- Vice President—Student Government   January 2013-December 2013

Figure 13-1. Resume with special projects section.

Should I Include Only Projects That Relate to the Job/Field I Am Applying for?

You are not limited to including projects related to the job/field you are applying for. However, if you include those outside of the job/field you are applying for, identify a transferrable skill you gained and include it with the description of what you accomplished in the special project.

The next chapter is going to cover how to include hobbies and interests in the resume.

Chapter 14

Optional Section: Hobbies and Interests

You may list some of your interests or hobbies as part of the resume. Although this section is purely optional, employers actually like to hire associates who are well-rounded and have interests outside of work. In addition, it might be to your benefit if you and the recruiter share a common hobby or interest, which can be a great conversation starter during the interview.

This section should be placed at the end of the resume and can be labeled as follows:

- Hobbies
- Interests
- Hobbies and Interests

Below are a few rules:

Rule 1: Only include the hobbies and interests section if you have enough room on the resume.

It is important to complete as many of the required sections of the resume before including the optional hobbies and interests section.

Rule 2: Avoid listing anything that could make you look bad or may be seen as negative by the public.

The following are a few examples of hobbies or interests that would **NOT** be appropriate to list on the resume:

- Pyrotechnics
- Stealing
- Internet dating
- Barhopping
- Women
- Men
- Smoking

Rule 3: Do NOT list interests/hobbies that are too generic.

Including interests and hobbies that are too generic will not provide the recruiter an accurate idea of your personality nor make you stand out. The left column of table 14.1 provides examples of what activities should **NOT** be listed on the resume because they are too generic. The right hand column lists interests/hobbies that are more specific and therefore of greater impact to the resume.

Table 14-1. Appropriate and inappropriate ways to describe your hobbies.

Hobbies That Are Too Generic for a Resume	Hobbies That Are More Specific/Impactful for a Resume
Traveling	Visiting new countries and experiencing new cultures
Exercising	Marathon running, Olympic weight lifting, yoga, cycling
Movies	Watching movies of a specific actor/actress, foreign films, comedies, action thrillers
Cooking	Gourmet cooking, grilling, Asian cuisine, exotic foods, Southern-comfort cooking
Dancing	Latin dancing, ballroom dancing, tap dance, contemporary dancing
Sports	Coaching little league soccer, basketball, racquet ball, football, tennis competitions
Music	Playing the flute, composing music, attending opera performances, jazz, reggae, hip-hop
Cars	Car restoration, watching professional car races, vintage cars

Fig. 14-1 provides an example of a resume that uses a hobbies and interests section.

MARCUS GROVER SMITH

23423 Lakeway Drive   *512-343-2090*
Austin, TX 78743   *Marcus.G.Smith@mail.com*

Objective   Dependable and adaptable leader with strong organizational and computing skills pursuing a job in business management within the financial services industry

Education   The University of Texas at Austin, McCombs School of Business   Austin, TX
Bachelor of Science in Business Administration   Minor: French
Tentative May 2014   **GPA:** 3.6

Honors   Yellow Rose scholar, Business National Honor Society, Junior of the Year

Skills   Proficient in Microsoft Office including Risk, StatTools, and PrecisionTree

Experience
June 2012—   **Equilat Business Solutions**   **Austin, TX**
Aug 2012   *Product Management Intern*
- Supported the product manager on competitive analysis of a new product
- Gained knowledge about demand and forecast tracking
- Reduced downtime of requirements gathering process by 24% as part of a product implementation improvement project (savings of $63K)
- Exhibited strong relationship building skills when working on teams

June 2011—   **Goodie Goods Food Brands**   **San Antonio, TX**
Sept 2011   *Operations Management Intern*
- Assisted operations manager with project execution tracking
- Reduced headcount expenses by 8% by performing data analysis on labor costs
- Demonstrated strong leadership when organizing deaf awareness week
- Prepared agendas for weekly team meetings

Leadership   President, Recycling in Austin Society   January 2011-present
Cycling Group   January 2011-December 2011
President, Business National Honor Society September 2010-May 2011

Interests   Camping, hiking, cycling, basketball, participating in local recycling programs

Travel   Mexico, Belize, Guatemala, Nicaragua, Costa Rica, Panama, Colombia, Peru

Languages   English and Spanish (fluent), French (4.5 years of study)

Figure 14-1. Resume with a hobbies and interests section.

The next chapter will illustrate how your resume should look and feel.

Chapter 15

The Resume's General Appearance

In the previous sections, we discussed the appropriate content for a resume. Now let's discuss general guidelines to improve its appearance.

Margins

One-inch margins should be used on the page to prevent the resume from appearing too crowded or empty.

Color

The text color should remain black throughout the resume. It is not necessary to add a color to the student's name in the attempt to make it stick out. The only exception is the e-mail address on an electronic resume, which when typed automatically gets a blue color and becomes underlined as a hyperlink. This format can be maintained if you are submitting it electronically. However, when printed, the e-mail address should remain in black color and not underlined.

The page used to print the resume should also be a clean, white standard 8.5"×11" sheet of paper, not other light-colored choices. White adds a professional look to the page.

Font

Times New Roman and Arial are the preferred fonts because they are the easiest to read. There are some instances, especially in the field of architecture, where it is encouraged to be more creative with the fonts. However, for most resumes, Times New Roman and Arial are the best font choices. Choose one and stick with it throughout the page.

Word Size

The letter size should be between 10 and 12. Any font size less than 10 is going to be too small and may result in recruiters not reading your resume, simply because they cannot read the words! Any font size larger than 12 is going to give your resume an unprofessional appearance. In addition, the recruiter will probably wonder if you used a font size greater than 12 just because you did not have enough content to fill out a whole page.

Recommendations: Create the first draft of the resume in size 11. Don't worry if you do not fill the page or if you exceed it. Just make sure you write what you can, taking into consideration the different guidelines mentioned in the previous chapters. If you find yourself not taking up the full page using size 11, then perhaps you should consider using size 12. In the same manner, if you find yourself exceeding one page, then you should consider using size 10. Also, make sure you stick to one font size. For example, the resume's content will not look right if you alternate back and forth between size 10 and 12. Below are a few exceptions to this rule:

- Your name can be 6 to 8 font sizes higher than the font size of the resume's content sections.
- The mailing address, phone number, and e-mail address can be 1 size lower than the font size of the resume's content sections.
- The subtitles of the different sections, such as work experience or education, can be 1 size higher than the font size of the content

Use of Bold, Italics, and Underline Options

Headers stand out in the resume when making them bold, italicized, and/or underlined. This will also ensure a cleaner and more professional appearance. Take a look at the following resume in fig. 15-1, which has been written without the use of bold, italics, and underline options. Then take a look at the resume in fig. 15-2 to observe how the use of bold, italics, and underlining improves its look.

PENELOPE PARKER

764 Yardey Drive
Athens, Georgia 45322

C: (618) 234-7392
Penelope.Parker@mail.com

Objective: Knowledgeable and vibrant college graduate with sales and decision-making skills seeking a job opportunity in event planning within the wedding industry

Education

The University of Colorado-College of Liberal Arts   Boulder, Colorado   GPA: 3.0
Bachelor of Arts in Journalism, Concentration in Public Relations   Minor: History   May 2010

Awards

- Top Revenue Generator 2007—A Day to Remember Weddings
- Recognized in Denver Wedding Association Annual Magazine as Intern of the Year 2009
- 2009 Top Event Coordinator—the University of Colorado

Work History

Sales Associate, Splash of Purple Inc.   Denver, CO   Sep. 2012-present

- Contribute to creative design of store layout through careful analysis of product placement
- Reduced customer wait times by proactively assisting in cash register during peak hours
- Used Excel, Word, and PowerPoint on a daily basis to produce vital customer documents

Event Coordinator, First Impressions LLC   Broomfield, CO   Nov. 2009-Aug. 2012

- Assembled tables, chairs, and linens and built exuberant and dramatic centerpieces
- Worked with caterers on selecting savory menu options and organizing meal logistics
- Performed extensive research to identify the best solutions for client-specific budgets

Intern, A Day to Remember Weddings LLC   Denver, CO   Jan. 2007-Aug. 2008

- Met with clients to assess wedding needs and understand nice-to-haves and must-haves
- Provided suggestions to help reduce costs while maintaining the customer's theme
- Delivered presentations at the Denver Wedding Convention to showcase company

Organization Involvement

- President   University of Colorado Communication Group   2010
- Vice President   Communication Society   2009
- Community Service Chair   Alpha Alpha Alpha Sorority   2008
- Cocaptain   Intramural soccer team   2007-2008

Languages: Fluent in spoken and written English and Spanish, Arabic (five years)

International Travel: Canada, Mexico, Nicaragua, France, Spain, Italy, Egypt, and Australia

Figure 15-1. Resume without the use of bold, italics, and underline options.

PENELOPE PARKER

764 Yardey Drive
Athens, Georgia 45322

C: (618) 234-7392
Penelope.Parker@mail.com

Objective: Knowledgeable and vibrant college graduate with sales and decision-making skills seeking a job opportunity in event planning within the wedding industry

Education

The University of Colorado-College of Liberal Arts   Boulder, Colorado   **GPA:** 3.0
Bachelor of Arts in Journalism, Concentration in Public Relations   Minor: History   May 2010

Awards

- Top Revenue Generator 2007—A Day to Remember Weddings
- Recognized in *Denver Wedding Association Annual Magazine* as Intern of the Year 2009
- 2009 Top Event Coordinator—the University of Colorado

Work History

Sales Associate, **Splash of Purple Inc.**   Denver, CO   Sep. 2012-present

- Contribute to creative design of store layout through careful analysis of product placement
- Reduced customer wait times by proactively assisting in cash register during peak hours
- Used Excel, Word, and PowerPoint on a daily basis to produce vital customer documents

Event Coordinator, **First Impressions LLC**   Broomfield, CO   Nov. 2009-Aug. 2012

- Assembled tables, chairs, and linens and built exuberant and dramatic centerpieces
- Worked with caterers on selecting savory menu options and organizing meal logistics
- Performed extensive research to identify the best solutions for client-specific budgets

Intern, **A Day to Remember Weddings LLC**   Denver, CO   Jan. 2007-Aug. 2008

- Met with clients to assess wedding needs and understand nice-to-haves and must-haves
- Provided suggestions to help reduce costs while maintaining the customer's theme
- Delivered presentations at the Denver Wedding Convention to showcase company

Organization Involvement

• President	University of Colorado Communication Group	2010
• Vice President	Communication Society	2009
• Community Service Chair	Alpha Alpha Alpha Sorority	2008
• Cocaptain	Intramural soccer team	2007-2008

Languages: Fluent in spoken and written English and Spanish, Arabic (five years)

International Travel: Canada, Mexico, Nicaragua, France, Spain, Italy, Egypt, and Australia

Figure 15-2. Resume with the use of bold, italics, and underline options.

Only One Page Needed

When I wrote my first resume in college, it was about four pages long. It included accomplishments since elementary school! When one of the seniors reviewed it, she told me that it needed to be only one page long, and I needed to focus on recent relevant accomplishments/experiences. In general, you want your resume to be no more than one page.

Why Am I Limited to Only One Page?

Recruiters and employers do not have time to read lengthy resumes. Your resume serves as a *marketing tool*. You do not want to include everything you have done in your entire life but just enough information so that an employer will be intrigued enough to offer you an interview. Remember, its purpose is to get you an interview. Once you have over ten years of significant post-college work experience, we can discuss whether or not more than one page is needed. But for now, one full page will suffice.

How Much Time Do Recruiters Spend Reading Individual Resumes?

Twenty minutes? Ten minutes? Five minutes? Guess again. Less than one minute! Yes, that is correct. Therefore, you have to make it as impressive as possible. Always include the most important items and keep it to only one page.

The 60/40 Rule

When looking at a resume, 60 percent of the piece of paper making up the resume should be filled with words in black, and

40 percent should be white space. This is the 60/40 rule. Having this balance of black words and white space on the resume will immediately send a positive message to the recruiter prior to reading the resume because it will seem more organized and professional. Let's look at a few examples.

What do you think about the resume in fig. 15-3?

Penelope Parker

764 Yardey Drive • Athens, Georgia 45322

C: (618) 234-7392

Penelope.Parker@mail.com

Qualifications

- Great professional demeanor
- Working knowledge of Excel, Word, and PowerPoint

Education

- The University of Colorado
- BA in communications

Work History

- Visual merchandise and sales associate
  Splash of Purple, Denver, Colorado

  September 2012-present

  - Assist customers and design the layout of the store

- Event coordinator
  First Impressions, Broomfield, Colorado

  November 2009 to August 2012

  - Organized weddings

Figure 15-3. Resume with about 15 percent black and 85 percent white.

As you can see, it has about 15 percent black and about 85 percent white. The first impression a recruiter will get when reading a resume that has as much white is that the candidate lacks experience. As a result, the recruiter will most likely not spend any time reading the resume. So the lesson here is to find enough skills, experiences, and accomplishments to fill one page with about 60 percent black and 40 percent white. This person could have also included a career objective, leadership skills, and even her hobbies or interests to take up more space.

Now what do you think about the following resume in fig. 15-4?

PENELOPE PARKER

764 Yardey Drive, Athens, Georgia 45322   C: (618) 234-7392   Penelope.Parker@mail.com

Objective: Knowledgeable and vibrant college graduate with sales and decision-making skills seeking a job opportunity in event planning within the wedding industry
Education: University of Colorado-College of Liberal Arts Boulder, Colorado **GPA:** 3.0 Bachelor of Arts in Journalism, Concentration in Public Relations **Minor:** History Grad Date: May 2010
Qualifications: Highly motivated, dedicated and ambitious professional; outstanding organizational and time management skills and strong attention to detail; successful in establishing and maintaining exceptional rapport with individuals on all levels; computer proficient in Microsoft Office: Excel, Word, PowerPoint, and Adobe InDesign
Awards: Top Revenue Generator 2007—A Day to Remember Weddings, recognized in *Denver Wedding Association Annual Magazine* as Intern of the Year, 2009 Top Event Coordinator—the University of Colorado, Junior of the Year—XYZ Department, full scholarship—University of Mississippi
Work History
Splash of Purple Denver, Colorado September 2012-present Visual merchandising and sales associate
Contribute to creative design of store layout through careful analysis of product placement
Exhibit great multitasking skills when consulting with customer requests while ensuring proper organization of inventory
Demonstrate professional demeanor when accepting payments for store merchandise
Ensure smooth flow of clients in the queue by proactively assisting in cash register during peak hours
Increase sales and customer delight by offering attractive clothing combinations to customers
Demonstrate strong reliability by always arriving to work early and adhering to company policies and procedures
Focus on developing team cohesiveness by always welcoming and coaching new associates in friendly manner
First Impressions Broomfield, Colorado November 2009-August 2012 Event coordinator
Assembled tables, chairs, and linens and built exuberant and dramatic centerpieces
Worked with caterers on selecting savory menu options and organizing meal logistics
Collaborated with vendors in a timely manner to guarantee proper execution of wedding, social event, and charity event deliverables
Performed extensive research to identify the best solutions for client-specific budgets
Provided strategic and elaborate floor layout of events to create inviting ambience and comfortable space
Coordinated bridal party activities and transportation to ensure proper schedule adherence
Helped construct chic invitations and delivered innovative favors for weddings
A Day to Remember Weddings Denver, Colorado January 2007-August 2008 *Intern*
Met with clients to assess wedding needs and understand nice-to-haves and must-haves
Guided clients through theme selection process, including but not limited to flower/centerpiece selection
Provided suggestions to help reduce costs while maintaining customer's theme
Delivered presentations at the Denver Wedding Convention to showcase company and increase sales
Organization Involvement: President, University of Colorado Communication Group 2010; Treasurer, Communications Honor Society 2009; Community Service Chair, Alpha Alpha Alpha Sorority 2008; Cocaptain, University of Colorado intramural soccer team 2007-2008
Hobbies: Yoga, SUP (stand up paddle), running marathons, rafting, opera, soccer, bird watching, theatre
Languages: Fluent in spoken and written English and Spanish, Arabic (five years)
International Travel: Canada, Mexico, Nicaragua, France, Spain, Italy, Egypt, Australia, New Zealand

Figure 15-4. Resume with too much black compared to the amount of white.

I'm sure you probably thought there was too much black compared to the amount of white. This is just as bad as not having enough on the resume because it looks so busy that it almost distracts from the content. A recruiter may choose not to read resumes that look busy or those that have more than 60 percent black.

In the resume that follows in fig. 15-5, good use of bullets and line spaces and keeping the most relevant information allow it to meet the 60/40 rule.

PENELOPE PARKER

764 Yardey Drive
Athens, Georgia 45322

C: (618) 234-7392
Penelope.Parker@mail.com

Objective: Knowledgeable and vibrant college graduate with sales and decision-making skills seeking a job opportunity in event planning within the wedding industry

Education

The University of Colorado-College of Liberal Arts   Boulder, Colorado   **GPA:** 3.0
Bachelor of Arts in Journalism, Concentration in Public Relations   Minor: History   May 2010

Awards
- Top Revenue Generator 2007—A Day to Remember Weddings
- Recognized in *Denver Wedding Association Annual Magazine* as Intern of the Year 2009
- 2009 Top Event Coordinator—the University of Colorado

Work History

Sales associate, **Splash of Purple Inc.**   Denver, CO   September 2012-present
- Contribute to creative design of store layout through careful analysis of product placement
- Reduced customer wait time by proactively assisting in cash register during peak hours
- Used Excel, Word, and PowerPoint on a daily basis to produce vital customer documents

Event coordinator, **First Impressions LLC**   Broomfield, CO   November 2009-August 2012
- Assembled tables, chairs, and linens and built exuberant and dramatic centerpieces
- Worked with caterers on selecting savory menu options and organizing meal logistics
- Performed extensive research to identify the best solutions for client-specific budgets

Intern, **A Day to Remember Weddings LLC**   Denver, CO   January 2007-August 2008
- Met with clients to assess wedding needs and understand nice-to-haves and must-haves
- Provided suggestions to help reduce costs while maintaining the customer's theme
- Delivered presentations at the Denver Wedding Convention to showcase company

Organization Involvement
- President   University of Colorado Communication Group   2010
- Vice president   Communication Society   2009
- Community service chair   Alpha Alpha Alpha Sorority   2008
- Cocaptain   Intramural soccer team   2007-2008

Languages: Fluent in spoken and written English and Spanish, Arabic (five years)

International Travel: Canada, Mexico, Nicaragua, France, Spain, Italy, Egypt, and Australia

---

Figure 15-5. Resume representing a good mix of black and white (the 60/40 rule).

Photographs/Graphics

It is not necessary to include any photographs or graphics on the resume. You want to make the best use of the amount of space you have for the required sections discussed in the earlier chapters.

Spelling and Grammar

Always ensure there are no misspellings or grammar errors on the resume. Once, I read a resume of someone who was applying for a management position. However, this person had the word *management* misspelled throughout the entire resume and had already turned it in to several recruiters. Needless to say, the person did not get an interview. Please make use of any spelling correction tools and ask someone to proofread your resume to avoid these silly mistakes. A misspelled word or incorrect grammar on the resume could result in not being invited to interview.

Submitting the Resume on the Internet or Online

Always attach your resume as a PDF file when e-mailing it to a recruiter. This will eliminate the chance of sending a Word file with the Track Changes option still on, a mistake many students make. When applying for a job through a company website, you will usually have the option to attach your resume or to copy and paste it. If you attach it, send it as a PDF file, and if you choose to copy and paste it, you should do the following:

- Replace all bullets with a plus (+) sign.
- Remove any physical lines.
- Convert all bold or italicized text to plain text.
- Align all text to the left.
- Capitalize all section headings.

Fig. 15-6 provides an example of a resume with these incorporated changes.

PENELOPE PARKER
764 Yardey Drive, Athens, Georgia 45322
C: (618) 234-7392
e-mail: Penelope.Parker@mail.com

OBJECTIVE
Knowledgeable and vibrant college graduate with sales and decision-making skills seeking a job opportunity in event planning within the wedding industry

EDUCATION
The University of Colorado-College of Liberal Arts, Boulder, Colorado, GPA: 3.0
Bachelor of Arts in Journalism, Concentration in Public Relations, Minor: History, May 2010

AWARDS
+ Top Revenue Generator 2007—A Day to Remember Weddings
+ Recognized in Denver Wedding Association Annual Magazine as Intern of the Year
+ 2009 Top Event Coordinator—the University of Colorado

WORK HISTORY

Sales associate, Splash of Purple   Denver, Colorado   September 2012-present
+ Contribute to creative design of store layout through careful analysis of product placement
+ Reduced customer wait time by proactively assisting in cash register during peak hours
+ Used Excel, Word, and PowerPoint on a daily basis to produce vital customer documents

Event coordinator, First Impressions   Broomfield, Colorado   November 2009-August 2012
+ Assembled tables, chairs, and linens and built exuberant and dramatic centerpieces
+ Worked with caterers on selecting savory menu options and organizing meal logistics
+ Performed extensive research to identify the best solutions for client-specific budgets

Intern, A Day to Remember Weddings   Denver, Colorado   January 2007-August 2008
+ Met with clients to assess wedding needs and understand nice-to-haves and must-haves
+ Provided suggestions to help reduce costs while staying within the customer theme
+ Delivered presentations at the Denver Wedding Convention to showcase company

ORGANIZATION INVOLVEMENT
+ President, University of Colorado Communication Group 2010
+ Treasurer, Communications Honor Society 2009
+ Community Service Chair, Alpha Alpha Alpha Sorority 2008
+ Cocaptain, Intramural soccer team 2007-2008

LANGUAGES: Fluent in spoken and written English and Spanish, Arabic (five years)

INTERNATIONAL TRAVEL: Canada, Mexico, Nicaragua, France, Spain, Italy, and Egypt

---

Figure 15-6. Formatted resume to copy and paste onto an online site.

The next chapter will provide several examples of superior resumes.

© 2007 Ted Goff

"Before we start the interview,
I know you'll want to read
the rest of my resume."

Chapter 16

Examples of Complete Resumes

Several examples of partial and complete resumes have been provided in the previous chapters. In this section, in addition to those, you will be able to review new resumes to give you a better idea of what the finished product should look like. As you will see, there is no specific template that must be used.

MARCIA EVANGELISTA LOPEZ

56543 Desert Trails Street
Albuquerque, NM 87001
325.969.4958
Marcia.Lopez@mail.com

OBJECTIVE

Enthusiastic and creative student with clever and impressive advertising ideas seeking a full time marketing role in the cosmetics industry

EDUCATION

University of New Mexico-Anderson School of Management   Albuquerque, NM
Bachelor of Arts in Marketing   Minor: Communications   Expected May 2014   **GPA 3.4**

QUALIFICATIONS

- Experienced in event coordination
- Efficient and organized
- Self-motivated
- Strong team player

- Creative communication (oral & written)
- Microsoft Access, Excel, PowerPoint, Word, Acrobat, Photoshop, Publisher, 65 WPM)

PROFESSIONAL EXPERIENCE

***Marketing Intern*-USA Marketing**   Albuquerque, NM   Summer 2012

- Paid close attention to detail when arranging travel and tracking vacation requests
- Scheduled bi-monthly marketing meetings and prepared agendas
- Assisted with development of marketing plan for new line of makeup
- Coordinated event for new product with 1K people in attendance & $25K in pre-sales

***Marketing Intern*-CDS&L Marketing Group**   Santa Fe, NM   Summer 2011

- Conducted market research on willingness to pay figures for a baby nutritional product
- Maintained account lists and client contacts for over 250 clients
- Demonstrated creativity when designing brochures and pamphlets

HONORS

- 1st place-University of New Mexico Marketing Case Competition, 2013
- National Honor Society-University of New Mexico Chapter, 2013
- Marketing Junior of the Year, 2013

EXTRACURRICULAR ACTIVITIES

- President-Anderson School of Management Marketing Club, 2013
- Secretary-Dance Society of New Mexico, 2013
- Member-Volleyball team, 2011-2012

CHRISTOPHER S. OWENS

9898 Persephone Hills Road
Montpelier, Vermont 23223
(254) 230-3465
Chistopher.Owens@mail.com

Objective
Accomplished and artistic individual with unique web design and typography skills seeking a full-time position as a graphic designer in the sports industry

Education
American University, College of Arts and Sciences   Washington, DC   GPA: 3.60
Bachelor of Arts in Graphic Design   Minor: French   Tentative 5/14

Technical Skills
- Autodesk AutoCAD
- Adobe Photoshop
- Adobe Illustrator
- Adobe Flash
- Dreamweaver HTML
- Microsoft Word
- Microsoft PowerPoint
- Microsoft Excel

Personal Strengths
- Exceptional written and oral communication and presentation skills
- Detail-oriented and excellent multitasking ability
- Excellent ability to maneuver through intricate organizational structures
- Strong ethical standards, reliability, and accountability

Work Experience
HJKE&R, Graphic Design Intern   Miami, Florida   January 2013-May 2013
- Explored different design typologies based on extensive survey data
- Gained experience working with cross-functional teams when developing new product marketing design
- Exemplified strong creativity when developing effective brochures, application kits, and flyers for clients

Leadership Skills
- August 2013-present, President of Graphic Design Student Association
- March 2012-May 2013, Banquet chair of Student Government Association
- January 2012-December 2012, Vice President of lacrosse team

Honors
- National Design Honor Society, January 2012-present
- 1st place—2012 American University Graphic Design Competition

Community Service Events
- Orange Fest, (2012 & 2013)—Organized a neighborhood festival to support a fun Halloween gathering for underprivileged youth
- Meals on Wheels, (2012)—Raised $6K to purchase food for the needy
- March of Dimes, (2012-2013)—Volunteered as the annual gala coordinator to celebrate the year's accomplishments
- Hurricane Charlie Fundraiser, (2013)—Raised $5K for a family who lost their house during Hurricane Charlie

Nicole R. Smith
12334 Long Shadow Street
New Orleans, Louisiana
934-265-5616
nicole.r.smith@mail.com

Objective

Talented and proactive undergraduate with strong business acumen and technical aptitude seeking a career in operations management in the agriculture industry

Education

California State University, Chico   College of Agriculture   Chico, California
Bachelor of Science in Agricultural Business   **GPA:** 3.8   Expected May 2014

Technical Skills

- Proficient in Microsoft Office Systems: Access, Excel, Outlook, PowerPoint, and Word
- Proficient in Agricultural systems: WinPig, ABECAS, AGRIS V9, ExtendAg, AgManager Package 4, AgCheck Accounting, PeachTree Accounting, and AgWorks

Employment

Labs XYZ Inc.

Operations Supervisor Intern   Phoenix, Arizona   June 2013-present

- Manage and maintain proper lab inventory levels through careful attention to detail
- Demonstrate responsibility when updating daily records and generating monthly reports for management
- Exemplify strong customer focus when working with suppliers and business partners
- Cared for livestock when administering preventive care

Leadership Roles

- President, Association of Agriculture Students   January 2012-present
- Member, University Cheerleading Association   August 2010-present
- Vice President, Association of Agriculture Students   January 2011-December 2011
- Secretary, Beta Beta Beta National Honor Society   August 2011-May 2012
- Vice President of Membership, Beta Beta Beta Sorority   August 2010-May 2011

Honors

- First Place winner—Agriculture Management Junior Project   December 2012
- Second Place—Sigma Sigma Sigma talent show   October 2012
- Junior of the Year, Association of Agriculture Students   May 2012
- Dean's Award finalist   April 2012
- Beta Beta Beta National Honor Society   August 2011-present

SOPHIA A. CANNON

2691 Saint Charles Avenue
Boston, MA 44009

(985) 372-8529
sofia.cannon@mail.com

OBJECTIVE

Energetic and driven individual with exceptional persuasion and listening skills seeking a sales opportunity in the computer hardware industry

EDUCATION

Boston University, School of Management   Boston, MA   Expected May 2014
Bachelor of Science in Business Administration   **GPA:** 4.0

SUMMARY OF QUALIFICATIONS

- Outstanding customer service and sales techniques
- Supportive and motivating team member
- Exceptional organizational skills for multiple task management and project completion
- Detail-oriented and excellent communication skills
- Proficient in QuickBooks 2007-2009, Quicken 2008, and Microsoft Office 2007

AWARDS

Platinum Award for Top Summer Intern—southeast region, 2012   Westcott Computers Inc.
Most Dedicated Volunteer of the Year, 2011   Hearts for the Homeless
National Society of Business Scholars inductee, 2011   Boston University

WORK EXPERIENCE

Westcott Computer Company

Sales Intern   Boston, MA   *June 2012-August 2012*

- Demonstrated strong financial acumen when forecasting daily sales and related costs
- Increased revenue of southeast region by 14% by negotiating computer sales contracts
- Utilized excellent communication skills when assisting clients in acquiring Westcott products
- Gained strong knowledge of sales policies and procedures when assisting sales manager
- Provided excellent customer service to clients in southeast region when creating work orders

EXTRACURRICULAR ACTIVITIES

- Treasurer, Sales Student Association—one year
- Secretary, Sales Student Association—one year
- President, Alpha Alpha Alpha National Sales Honor Society—one year

COMMUNITY SERVICE

- Hearts for the Homeless, 2011
- Recycling Friends of America, 2012

LAWRENCE BENICIO MARTINEZ

5620 Glenloaf Drive   *713-339-4949*
Sugarland, TX 77391   *LBMartinez@yahoo.com*

OBJECTIVE: Dedicated and well-organized individual with excellent leadership and technical skills seeking a computer engineering role within the information technology industry

EDUCATION

University of Houston, Cullen College of Engineering   Houston, TX   **GPA: 3.86**
Bachelor of Science in Computer Engineering   Minor: Math   Expected May 2013

WORK EXPERIENCE

Computer World Inc.   Plano, TX   May 2012-August 2012
Computer Engineering Intern

- Reduced data collection time by 15% by introducing new online system for storing data
- Improved quality of testing by introducing two new testing procedures
- Gained valuable experience in writing scripts when assisting teams in planning project's testing phase

Chips and Dip Inc.   El Paso, TX   June 2011-September 2011
Computer Engineering Intern

- Acquired working knowledge of customer network maintenance when shadowing team
- Lessened catalogue content update time by designing code to automate vendor changes
- Exemplified strong communication skills when presenting to executive leadership team

ACADEMIC AWARDS, ACHIEVEMENTS, AND HONORS

- Most Outstanding Computer Engineering Junior, 2013
- 2011 Brother of the Year, Beta Beta Beta International Fraternity Inc.
- Induction into Sigma Sigma Sigma Computer Engineering National Honor Society, 2009

TECHNICAL SKILLS

Pascal, Fortran, Mathcad, Microsoft Office, Matlab, Control System, Simulation, Linux, Agile

ORGANIZATIONAL INVOLVEMENT AND LEADERSHIP ROLES

- President (one year)   Delta Delta National Leadership Honor Society
- President (two years)   Hispanic Student Association
- Vice President (one year)   Helping Hand (community service-related club)
- Vice President (six months)   Sigma Sigma Sigma National Honor Society
- Membership director (one year)   Institute of Computer Engineering Students
- District officer (one year)   Beta Beta Beta International Fraternity Inc.
- Principal violinist (three years)   University of Houston symphony orchestra
- Treasurer (one year)   University of Houston golf team

SANFORD JENKINS

4578 Yellow Bud Street
Las Vegas, NV 78759

957-326-3956
sanford.jenkins@mail.com

Objective
Collaborative and influential individual with positive and team-oriented personality pursuing an opportunity in higher-education administration

Education
University of Nevada-Las Vegas, College of Liberal Arts   Las Vegas, NV
Bachelor of Arts in Political Science, Minor: English
Expected May 2015   **GPA: 3.81**

Technical Skills
Microsoft Word, Excel, PowerPoint, Access, Outlook, Visio, Mac OS X

Work Experience
Nevada Bank
Teller   *Las Vegas, NV*   *August 2011-July 2013*
- Demonstrated strong oral communication skills when assisting customers with everyday banking needs
- Assisted team members during peak hours to promote a cohesive team environment and reduce wait times by 50%
- Provided exceptional customer service when operating cash drawer for commercial window
- Resolved customer complaints by using active listening skills and reacting quickly

Community Involvement
- Raised $1,305 as team captain for Women's Society and $2,385 as team captain for Asthma Society of Nevada, 2014
- Led a political science workshop for youth during college day, 2012 and 2013
- Volunteered for Libraries of Kids, Nevada Food Bank, and Las Vegas Community Center, 2013

Awards
- 2013 Silver Star Award for outstanding customer service at Nevada Bank
- 2012 Silver Star Award for outstanding customer service at Nevada Bank
- 2012 Leadership Excellence Award, University of Nevada—Las Vegas Student Organization Council

Leadership Roles
- President of Politics Honor Society, 2012-2013
- Secretary of Sigma Sigma Sigma International Fraternity Inc., 2011-2012

PENELOPE PARKER

764 Yardey Drive   *C: (618) 234-7392*
Athens, Georgia 45322   *Penelope.Parker@mail.com*

Objective: Knowledgeable and vibrant college graduate with sales and decision-making skills seeking a job opportunity in event planning within the wedding industry

Education

The University of Colorado-College of Liberal Arts   Boulder, Colorado   **GPA:** 3.0
Bachelor of Arts in Journalism, Concentration in Public Relations   Minor: History   May 2010

Awards

- Top Revenue Generator 2007—A Day to Remember Weddings
- Recognized in *Denver Wedding Association Annual Magazine* as Intern of the Year 2009
- 2009 Top Event Coordinator—the University of Colorado

Work History

Sales Associate, **Splash of Purple Inc.**   Denver, CO   Sept. 2012-present

- Contribute to creative design of store layout through careful analysis of product placement
- Reduced customer wait time by proactively assisting in cash register during peak hours
- Used Excel, Word, and PowerPoint on a daily basis to produce vital customer documents

Event Coordinator, **First Impressions LLC**   Broomfield, CO   Nov. 2009-Aug. 2012

- Assembled tables, chairs, and linens and built exuberant and dramatic centerpieces
- Worked with caterers on selecting savory menu options and organizing meal logistics
- Performed extensive research to identify the best solutions for client-specific budgets

Intern, **A Day to Remember Weddings LLC**   Denver, CO   Jan. 2007-Aug. 2008

- Met with clients to assess wedding needs and understand nice-to-haves and must-haves
- Provided suggestions to help reduce costs while maintaining the customer's theme
- Delivered presentations at the Denver Wedding Convention to showcase company

Organization Involvement

- President   University of Colorado Communication Group   2010
- Vice President   Communication Society   2009
- Community Service Chair   Alpha Alpha Alpha Sorority   2008
- Cocaptain   Intramural soccer team   2007-2008

Languages: Fluent in spoken and written English and Spanish, Arabic (five years)

International Travel: Canada, Mexico, Nicaragua, France, Spain, Italy, Egypt, and Australia

SUSAN MARIE CHEN

301 West Elm Road
Charlotte, NC 44356

445-367-6678
Susan.Chen12@mail.com

OBJECTIVE

Cosmopolitan and competent student with excellent oral and written communication skills seeking a public relations internship in the telecommunication industry

EDUCATION

University of Georgia, Franklin College of Arts and Science   Athens, GA   **GPA:** 3.6
Bachelor of Arts in Communication Studies   Minor: Theatre   Expected December 2014

SKILLS

- Proficient in Microsoft Office Systems: Access, Excel, Outlook, PowerPoint, and Word
- Ability to write press releases and promotional materials
- Skillful in developing computer graphics techniques for media productions

WORK EXPERIENCE

August 2012-present   **Ventura Inc.**   **Charleston, SC**
Executive Assistant

- Perform all administrative tasks such as preparing executive presentations, scheduling travel arrangements, and ordering office supplies for the vice president of sales
- Introduced the office recycling program to contribute to Ventura's culture of sustainability-site was recognized as green office of the week by Charleston KXRU radio station
- Organize team-spirit activities such as monthly potlucks as the chair of the spirit committee
- Maintain company organized by conducting expense reimbursement duties for the site

AWARDS

- Recipient of Brilliance Award at the Freshman Fundraising Competition ($23K)
- Induction into Communications Honor Society, 2012
- Winner of the Media Production Program Member of the Year award, 2011

LEADERSHIP ROLES

- Treasurer   Communications Society of America   January 2013-present
- Team captain   Intramural basketball   February 2012-January 2013
- Active member   Communities for Georgia   March 2011-December 2011

INTERNATIONAL TRAVEL

- Mexico
- Costa Rica
- Panama
- Venezuela
- France
- Spain
- The Netherlands
- Egypt
- Thailand
- China
- Australia
- New Zealand
- Singapore
- Vietnam
- Russia

PREETHA A. SANCHEZ

301 West Elm Road   *445-367-6678*
Oakland, CA 44356   *Preetha.Sanchez@mail.com*

OBJECTIVE

Sharp and confident student with design and marketing skills seeking a full time position in print and digital journalism within the international affairs broadcasting industry

EDUCATION

University of Southern California, Annenberg School for Communication and Journalism
Bachelor of Arts in Print and Digital Journalism   Los Angeles, CA   Tentative 12/14

SKILLS

Proficient in Microsoft Office Systems: Access, Excel, Outlook, PowerPoint, and Word

EXPERIENCE

June 2013-August 2013   **BCS Communication Group Inc.**   **Woodland Hills, CA**
Journalism Intern

- Gained exposure to executive leadership team when performing administrative tasks for the CEO/president of company
- Showed strong planning skills when coordinating media/promotional tours and regional programs and events
- Exemplified effective administration skills when scheduling meetings with clients and preparing strategic meeting agendas

June 2012-August 2012   **Coastal Products Limited**   **San Francisco, CA**
Advertising/Marketing Intern

- Showcased superior design skills when creating attractive page layouts for monthly publications
- Edited English documents daily and translated them to Spanish for Latin American clients
- Used adequate diplomacy when representing the company at the annual Coastal Technology Conference

HONORS

Second Place—Regionals Swim Team (2012), Third Place—Regionals Swim Team (2011)

CLUB INVOLVEMENT

Indian Media Association, Journalism Society, university swim team, Beta Beta Beta Sorority

INTERNATIONAL TRAVEL

India, Mexico, Peru, Argentina, Canada, Iceland, Thailand, Japan, Singapore, England, France

LANGUAGES

English (fluent), standard Hindi (fluent), Spanish (advanced), Japanese (three years)

MARCUS GROVER SMITH

23423 Lakeway Drive   512-343-2090
Austin, TX 78743   Marcus.G.Smith@mail.com

Objective Dependable and adaptable leader with strong organizational and computing skills pursuing a job in business management within the financial services industry

Education The University of Texas at Austin, McCombs School of Business   Austin, TX
Bachelor of Science in Business Administration   Minor: French
Tentative May 2014   **GPA:** 3.6

Honors Yellow Rose scholar, Business National Honor Society, Junior of the Year

Skills Proficient in Microsoft Office including Risk, StatTools, and PrecisionTree

Experience
June 2012— **Equilat Business Solutions**   **Austin, TX**
Aug 2012 *Product Management Intern*

- Supported the product manager on competitive analysis of a new product
- Gained knowledge about demand and forecast tracking
- Reduced downtime of requirements gathering process by 24% as part of a product implementation improvement project—savings of $63K
- Exhibited strong relationship building skills when working on teams

June 2011— **Goodie Goods Food Brands**   **San Antonio, TX**
Sept 2011 *Operations Management Intern*

- Assisted operations manager with project execution tracking
- Reduced headcount expenses by 8% by performing data analysis on labor costs
- Demonstrated strong leadership when organizing deaf awareness week
- Prepared agendas for weekly team meetings

Leadership President, Recycling in Austin Society   January 2011-present
Cycling Group   January 2011-December 2011
President, Business National Honor Society   September 2010-May 2011

Interests Camping, hiking, cycling, basketball, participating in local recycling programs

Travel Mexico, Belize, Guatemala, Nicaragua, Costa Rica, Panama, Colombia, Peru

Languages English and Spanish (fluent), French (4.5 years of study)

RUBEN BRYAN ARMSTRONG

4800 Long Meadow Street   *704-345-6789*
Charlotte, NC 23456   *Ruben.Armstrong@mail.com*

Career Objective

Dynamic and innovative student with exceptional analytical and modeling skills searching for an industrial engineering internship within the airline industry

Education

The University of Houston-Cullen College of Engineering   Houston, TX   **GPA:** 3.75
Bachelor of Science in Industrial Engineering   Minor: Business   Expected May 2014

Special Projects

- *XYZ Company Workstation Ergonomic Improvements*—(class: Human Factors)—provided ergonomic improvement recommendations by performing analysis on workstations
- *Traffic Light Vibration Reduction*—(class: Design IV)—decreased traffic light post vibrations by designing and constructing four dampers
- *Rainbow Airlines Ticket Counter Optimization*—(class: Simulation)—reduced customers' wait times by collecting data on ticket counter check-in process

Work Experience

June 2013-August 2013   HRS&T Steel Manufacturing LLC   Alvin, Texas
Industrial Engineering Intern

- Reduced overall scrap by 23% by performing time studies on key manufacturing processes
- Gained relevant knowledge on safety methodologies when assisting the operations manager
- Obtained vital presentation skills when delivering project results to the plant's director
- Created scorecard for evaluating productivity and quality goals

Awards

- Cullen College of Engineering Design Competition, 2nd place winner   2013
- La Hacienda Twenty-fifth Anniversary Scholarship recipient   2013
- Officer of the Year, Student Government   2012

Leadership Roles and Organizational Involvement

- President—Alpha Industrial Engineering Honor Society   May 2013-present
- Vice President—Student Government   January 2013-December 2013
- Parliamentarian—Student Government   January 2012-December 2012

ABDUL MUHAMMAD KHALIL

9999 Great Meadows Lane
Providence, Rhode Island 22222
(555)-555-5555
Abdul.M.Khalil@mail.com

Objective

Compassionate and acute student with great interpersonal and leadership skills pursuing an internship in social work

Education

University of Louisville   Louisville, KY
College of Arts and Sciences
Bachelor of Arts in Psychology   Minor: German   Expected May 2016

Experience
Summer 2014

Jacobi Orphanage   Louisville, Kentucky
Summer Intern

- Created an organized work environment by assisting case manager with filing patient records
- Acquired critical interpersonal skills when conducting patient interviews
- Led implementation of the Sunshine Kids Information Initiative

Summer 2013

Alberto Hinojosa Elementary School   Louisville, Kentucky
Counselor Assistant

- Demonstrated intellectual agility by identifying process gaps, resulting in 60%decline in lost student paperwork
- Exemplified leadership when counseling at-risk students
- Showed leadership skills when organizing College Day

Leadership

2014   President, Psychology Student Association
2013   Community Service chair, Chi Chi Chi International Fraternity Inc.

Awards

2014   Member of the Month (December), Psychology Student Association
2013   Member of the Month (July), Student Government
2013   Community Service Award, Chi Chi Chi International Fraternity Inc

Interests

Competing in judo tournaments, coaching little league football, scuba diving, rock climbing, volunteering at the Katz Burn Center

HERBERT BROWN

64903 Oak Meadow Street
Dallas, TX 34579
342-543-3655
Herbert.Brown34@mail.com

OBJECTIVE

Self-motivated and detail-oriented graduate with computing and analytical skills looking for a laboratory technologist position within the pharmaceutical industry

EDUCATION

University of Southern California-Dornsife College of Letters, Arts, and Sciences
Bachelor of Science in Chemistry   Los Angeles, CA   08/2012-05/2016   **GPA: 3.7**
Recipient of the Chemistry Brilliance Award, 2015

SUMMARY OF QUALIFICATIONS

- Exceptional knowledge in MS Word, Excel, and PowerPoint
- Excellent communication and analytical skills
- Ability to analyze and interpret technical reports

WORK EXPERIENCE

Lab Operator, **ABC Chemicals Inc.**   06/2016-present   Broussard, Louisiana

- Ensure compliance with quality standards by performing daily lab inspections
- Pay close attention to detail when preparing lab samples for corporate clients
- Improve product output by performing proactive maintenance of lab equipment
- Develop and maintain database to accurately record and track defect trends

ORGANIZATIONAL INVOLVEMENT

- Secretary for the Association of Campus Leaders, 08/2014-04/2015
- Treasurer for the Annual Homecoming Festival, 01/2014-10/2014
- Membership Coordinator for the Mathematics Honor Society, 08/2013-05/2014

LANGUAGES

English (fluent), Spanish (four years), Arabic (four years)

COMMUNITY INVOLVEMENT

- Volunteered at the Annual Dallas Thanksgiving Dinner-November 2013
- Donated 250 toys by spearheading Children Christmas Toy Drive-December 2014
- Raised funds for construction of playground in Lancaster Park-September 2015

PETER ALEXANDER DANIELIAN

9999 Stonelake Boulevard
Orlando, FL 23456
876-345-6789
Peter.Danielian@mail.com

Career Objective

Friendly and professional finance undergraduate with problem solving and interpersonal communication skills looking for a finance position in the real estate industry

Education

University of Central Florida, College of Business Administration   Orlando, FL
Bachelor of Arts in Finance   Minor: Management   Expected May 2016   **GPA:** 3.35

Work Experience

Computer World Inc.   Naples, FL   August 2014-August 2015
Finance Assistant

- Collaborated with members of the finance team to assess proper reconciliation of accounts
- Demonstrated strong technical skills when utilizing internal databases to create monthly financial reports
- Reduced customer complaints by 25% by preparing work instructions to a key customer-facing process
- Collected weekly data for finance manager to enhance revenue of product base

Phone Land LLC   Miami, FL   June 2013-August 2014
Management Assistant

- Conducted credit history reviews to evaluate and approve new accounts
- Exemplified teamwork when coordinating customer questions with sales representatives
- Eliminated labor costs by 10% by creating daily reconciliation process

Leadership

- Vice president, Campus Crusaders, August 2014-April 2015
- Membership Chair, Finance Student Organization, January 2014-October 2014
- Social Chair, Nu Nu Nu Fraternity, August 2013-May 2014

Awards

- Daniel A. Riley Campus Crusaders Leadership Award-September 2014
- Member of the Year, Finance Student Organization-September 2015

Languages

English (fluent), German (fluent), French (advanced), Greek (four years)

The next chapter provides an easy, step-by-step approach to create a cover letter, including samples for you to view as well.

Chapter 17

Tips for Writing a Cover Letter

Imagine you just completed your winning resume and are feeling more confident than ever. You decide to apply for that internship or dream job when all of a sudden you get stumped by the application. You are required to include a cover letter and don't even know what that is! No need to worry. This chapter will explain all you need to know about this requirement.

> A cover letter is a one-page formal letter to the company that summarizes why you are interested in and qualified for the job you are applying for.

It is different from the resume and is made up of the following components:

- The header
- Introductory paragraph
- The body
- Closing paragraph
- The farewell

Before we go into the details of each component, fig. 17-1 is an example of a cover letter.

May 6, 2013

Arrow Energy Corporation
4444 Raceway Street
Oakland, California 94583

Dear Hiring Manager:

I am a finance major and senior at the University of Oklahoma, where through careers services I learned about the Arrow Energy Finance Associate position. Since then, I had the opportunity to speak to April Martinez, business analyst for the Energy Finance Department at your institution, who encouraged me to apply. I am interested in gaining valuable knowledge working in energy finance in a respectable company such as yours. I believe that my experiences with leading student organizations, knowledge gained as an energy finance teacher's assistant, and a strong drive to work in a global and fast-paced business environment make me the perfect candidate.

Last summer, I worked for Heathrow Bank as a finance intern. During that time, I gained experience with data analysis, specifically in the fields of revenue and supply cost. At the end of the term, my team won third place at the end-of-year presentation to the executive leadership group. During the fall of my senior year, I took an energy finance class, which really excited me about working in an energy finance role. Prior to the end of the fall semester, I applied to be the spring semester teacher's assistant for the energy finance professor. I received the position and have been using this semester to refine my energy finance knowledge.

Working in your agency in the capacity of energy finance associate would be a great opportunity that would allow me to enhance my finance skills. Knowledge gained through my energy finance class, past experiences in other finance-related roles, and my effective communication skills would prove beneficial in this role. I have enclosed my resume for your perusal. Please feel free to contact me if you have any questions. I appreciate your consideration for this position.

Sincerely,

Nate Hollister
12322 Lansing Drive
Norman, OK 78222
Nate.Hollister@mail.com
(409) 455-4555

Figure 17-1. Sample cover letter.

Now that you have seen an example of a cover letter, let's review the different components in more detail.

The Header

The header is located at the top of the cover letter and is made up of the following components:

- The current date
- The company address
- The salutation

The Current Date

The current date is the date you are sending the cover letter to the company. In most instances, the cover letter would be sent electronically whenever you apply for the position online. If today's date is February 24, 2014, and you are sending the letter today or applying for the role today, then you would write this date at the top left of your cover letter. Always spell out the month's full name.

The Company Address

Write the company's name and headquarters' address at the top left of the letter. Below is an example:

Houser & Houser Inc.
2222 Troutser Lane
Phoenix, AZ 77777

In the event that you know the name and title of the person to whom you will be sending the cover letter, write both, separated by a comma, right above the address. Below is an example:

Aseemita Ramaswami, Director of Education
Houser & Houser Inc.
2222 Troutser Lane
Phoenix, AZ 77777

The Salutation

The salutation should be placed three lines below the last line of the company address. If you know the name of the person who will be receiving the cover letter, then you can make the salutation in his or her name using the correct suffix. Otherwise, use a general salutation. Table 17-1 below provides some examples of appropriate salutations:

Table 17-1. Salutations appropriate for a cover letter.

Salutation Format	Example
General	Dear Hiring Manager, Dear Hiring Officer:
Last name only	Dear Mr. Smith, Dear Ms. Hernandez: Dear Dr. Feng:
First and last name	Dear Mr. Everett Smith, Dear Ms. Melissa Hernandez: Dear Dr. Russell Feng:

Introductory Paragraph

The introductory paragraph should be placed three lines below the salutation and is made up of the following components:

- One or two sentences describing the following:

  o The year in school you are in (e.g., freshman, sophomore, junior, senior)
  o Your major
  o Your school's name
  o The position you are applying for
  o How you became familiar with the job posting

- One (or two) sentences describing why you are interested in the role
- One (or two) sentences explaining why you like the company
- One (or two) sentences describing why you are the perfect candidate for the job

Let's review these components in more detail using three examples from three different students: an African studies major, a chemistry major, and a political science major.

Year in School, Major, Name of School, Position's Name, and How the Posting Was Identified

The first sentence of the introductory paragraph of the cover letter should include the student's year in school, major, name of school, name of role, and how the job was identified, as you can see in the examples that follow:

Example 1—African studies major

I am a sophomore African studies major at Ohio University and recently heard about the African studies teaching assistant position from the African studies program's bulletin board.

Example 2—chemistry major

I am a junior studying chemistry at the University of Miami and became aware of the Chemistry Department's summer internship through _Dr. Allan Spellman,_ professor of organic chemistry at the University of Miami, who encouraged me to apply.

Example 3—political science major

I am a _senior political science major_ at the _University of North Carolina at Chapel Hill_ and read about the _social statistics associate_ opportunity in your _company website's careers section._

(For your convenience, I underlined specific words in the examples above and throughout the remaining examples below. However, do not underline these words on your cover letter).

Why Are You Interested in the Job?

In the second sentence of the introductory paragraph, explain briefly why you are applying for the role by listing the skills or work experiences you are hoping to gain. Below are a few examples:

Example 1—African studies major

I am a sophomore African studies major at Ohio University and recently heard about the African studies teaching assistant position from the African studies program's bulletin board. _I am interested in applying for this role to gain valuable experience working with an African studies professor, who can provide me with additional insight in this field of study._

Example 2—chemistry major

I am a junior studying chemistry at the University of Miami and became aware of the Chemistry Department's summer internship through Dr. Allan Spellman, professor of organic chemistry at the University of Miami, who encouraged me to apply. _This summer internship would allow me to apply the knowledge gained in my chemistry courses and most recent field study to continue to enhance my geochemistry skills._

Example 3—political science major

I am a senior political science major at the University of North Carolina at Chapel Hill and read about the social statistics associate opportunity in your company website's careers section. This position is important to me because it would give me working knowledge of how data can be used to influence political strategy.

Why Do You Like the Company (or Hiring Organization)?

In the third sentence of the introductory paragraph, explain briefly why you like the company (or hiring organization). There may be an award that the company won that really impressed you, or you may just be really interested in what you have heard about the company's culture. Below are a few examples explaining why you want to work in the company (or hiring organization):

Example 1—African studies major

I am a sophomore African studies major at Ohio University and recently heard about the African studies teaching assistant position from the African studies program's bulletin board. I am interested in applying for this role to gain valuable experience working with an African studies professor, who can provide me with additional insight in this field of study. In addition, the African studies program was ranked best in the nation this past year.

Example 2—chemistry major

I am a junior studying chemistry at the University of Miami and became aware of the Chemistry Department's summer internship through Dr. Allan Spellman, professor of organic chemistry, who encouraged me to apply. This summer internship would allow me to apply the knowledge gained in my chemistry courses and most recent field study to continue to enhance my geochemistry skills. <u>*The Chemistry Department's two month summer excursion makes it one of the strongest in the world.*</u>

Example 3—political science major

I am a senior political science major at the University of North Carolina at Chapel Hill and read about the social statistics associate opportunity in your company website's careers section. This position is important to me because it would give me working knowledge of how data can be used to influence political strategies. <u>*I was pleased to learn that Grover Sampson Consulting was ranked number 1 recently for employee satisfaction and number 1 for client success rate.*</u>

Why Are You the Best Job Candidate?

In the last sentence of the introductory paragraph, you will mention the top one to three reasons why you are the best job candidate. You can do this by providing skills and experiences you possess that are required and/or preferred for the role you are applying for. Below are a few examples:

Example 1—African studies major

I am a sophomore African studies major at Ohio University and recently heard about the African studies teaching assistant position from the African studies program's bulletin board. I am interested in applying for this role to gain valuable experience working with an African studies professor, who can provide me with additional insight in this field of study. In addition, the African studies program was ranked best in the nation this past year. <u>*I believe I am the best candidate for this role because of my academic achievement as an African studies major, my leadership skills, and my passion for educating others on African culture and history.*</u>

Example 2—chemistry major

I am a junior studying chemistry at the University of Miami and became aware of the Chemistry Department's summer internship through Dr. Allan Spellman, professor of organic chemistry, who encouraged me to apply. This summer internship would allow me to apply the knowledge gained in my chemistry courses and most recent field study to continue to enhance my geochemistry skills. The Chemistry Department's two month summer excursion makes it one of the strongest in the world. <u>I would excel greatly in this summer internship because of my significant analytical aptitude, drive for results, and proven success working in geochemistry teams.</u>

Example 3—political science major

I am a senior political science major at the University of North Carolina at Chapel Hill and read about the social statistics associate opportunity in your company website's careers section. This position is important to me because it would give me working knowledge of how data can be used to influence political strategies. I was pleased to learn that Grover Sampson Consulting was recently ranked number 1 for employee satisfaction and number 1 for client success rate. <u>My past experiences in analyzing large amounts of data, volunteering in two different political campaigns, and having the ability to learn quickly make me the perfect candidate for this role.</u>

Body of the Cover Letter

The paragraph following the introductory paragraph is referred to as the body and is a chronological summary of your past experiences and skills gained, making you qualified for the position. You are able to provide more detail in the body than you were in the introductory paragraph, and the body should start three lines below it. The key here is *not* to copy what you have on your resume word for word but to highlight the work experience and skills that makes you qualified for the role. Please see the following examples:

Example 1—African studies major

When I was a teenager, I saw a movie on different African countries, which sparked my interest in Africa's diverse cultures and history. I was very fortunate to take various trips with my family and church group to different African countries during a five-year period. Once I started college in the fall of 2013, I knew I wanted to major in African studies. Through the African studies program here on campus, I have had the opportunity to take additional trips to Egypt, Morocco, Nigeria, South Africa, Kenya, Angola, and Madagascar. My ultimate goal is to earn a doctorate so that I can teach African studies at the university level.

Example 2—chemistry major

The second semester of my freshman year in college, I was ranked number 1 in my chemistry class. As a result, in my sophomore year, I had the chance to serve as the chemistry professor's assistant in a freshman chemistry lab. Participating in a project led by my professor exposed me further to chemistry concepts, lab terminology, and most importantly, to the field of geochemistry. My professor invited me and a few other students to take a week-long field trip to an abandoned mine where we performed rock analysis. Our team presented our findings at the Annual Geochemistry Conference in Aspen earlier this year and received an award for our efforts.

Example 3—political science major

I became interested in political science during my freshman year when a friend and I decided to volunteer for Rebecca de la Cruz's city council campaign in Charlotte, North Carolina. I was primarily in charge of supporting the technology manager with the website and database. In addition, I assisted with data analysis of telecommunication costs associated with the campaign. De la Cruz's landslide victory motivated me to volunteer during my sophomore year for Dana Hillsworth's senatorial campaign in North Carolina. In this role, I supported the phone bank coordinator in ensuring that operations ran smoothly and learned a great deal about technology's impact on gaining more votes.

Closing Paragraph

The cover letter's closing paragraph consists of three to four sentences meant to wrap up the letter and should start three lines below the body paragraph. Here you will do the following:

- Emphasize why *the job* is a good fit for you
- Emphasize why *you* are a good fit for the job
- Thank the hiring manager for considering you for the job
- Express that you look forward to their response

Below are a few examples:

Example 1—African studies major

The African studies teaching assistant role would be an ideal opportunity for me to continue enhancing the knowledge I have gained through my coursework and travel. My enthusiasm for Africa's rich culture and history and proven track record within this program would make me a strong teacher's assistant. Thank you for considering me for this position. I have included my resume for your review, and I look forward to your response.

Example 2—chemistry major

The Chemistry Department's summer internship would provide me a chance to continue learning more about the field of geochemistry. If selected, I am confident that my accomplishments in the Chemistry Department and within geochemistry in the last few years have given me a strong foundation. Please feel free to call me if you have further questions. Thank you for your consideration, and I look forward to your reply.

Example 3—political science major

This position is ideal for me because it will allow me to gain experience in political strategy. I am a solid candidate for this role given my experience in data analysis and participation in campaign operations. Attached is my resume. Do not hesitate to contact me if you have any questions, and I hope you will consider me for the role. I look forward to hearing from you.

The Farewell

The cover letter's farewell follows the closing paragraph and contains the following components:

- The valediction
- Your name
- Your contact information

The Valediction

The valediction is the official farewell of the cover letter and is written three lines below the closing paragraph. Examples of appropriate valedictions are as follows:

- Sincerely,
- Thanks,
- Thank you,
- Cordially,
- Regards,
- Best regards,
- Warm regards,

Your Name

Type your name four lines under the valediction and as it appears on your resume. For example, if you listed your name as Katrina S. Chung on the resume, you should also write Katrina S. Chung on the cover letter. You do not need to sign your name on the cover letter if you are sending it electronically. Typing your name is sufficient in this case.

Your Contact Information

Below your name, list your contact information, which includes your mailing address, e-mail address, and phone number. Use the same contact information that appears on your resume on the cover letter.

Font

Like in the resume, you should stick with Times New Roman or Arial font with a letter size no smaller than size 10 and no bigger than size 12. Using a justified paragraph layout will also give you the cleanest look. You are not required to fill the entire page but should make sure not to exceed one page.

Complete Cover Letters

Using the examples from this chapter, fig. 17-2, fig. 17-3, and fig. 17-4 represent the three cover letters in their entirety:

December 4, 2014

Ohio University
Department of African Studies
4333 Bolivar Boulevard
Lancaster, OH 70802

Dear Hiring Manager:

I am a sophomore African studies major at Ohio University and recently heard about the African studies teaching assistant position from the African studies program's bulletin board. I am interested in applying for this role to gain valuable experience working with an African studies professor who can provide me with additional insight in this field of study. In addition, the African studies program was ranked best in the nation this past year. I believe I am the best candidate for this role because of my academic achievement as an African studies major, my leadership skills, and my passion for educating others on African culture and history.

When I was a teenager, I saw a movie on different African countries, which sparked my interest in Africa's diverse cultures and history. I was very fortunate to take various trips with my family and church group to different African countries during a five-year period. Once I started college in the fall of 2013, I knew I wanted to major in African studies. Through the African studies program here on campus, I have had the opportunity to take additional trips to Egypt, Morocco, Nigeria, South Africa, Kenya, Angola, and Madagascar. My ultimate goal is to earn a doctorate so that I can teach African studies at the university level.

The African studies teaching assistant role would be an ideal opportunity for me to continue enhancing the knowledge I have gained thus far through my course work and travel. My enthusiasm for Africa's rich culture and history and proven track record in this program would make me a strong teaching assistant. Thank you for considering me for this position. I have included my resume for your review and look forward to your response.

Regards,

Solana Escobar
2323 Sungate Lane
Lancaster, OH 70845
Solana.Escobar@mail.com
756-342-3343

Figure 17-2. African studies major's cover letter.

June 4, 2014

Mohan Patel, Professor of Geochemistry
University of Miami
Room 3, Box 8
5655 Main Street
Miami, FL 77832

Dear Dr. Patel:

I am a junior studying chemistry at the University of Miami and became aware of the Chemistry Department's summer internship through Dr. Allan Spellman, professor of organic chemistry, who encouraged me to apply. This summer internship would allow me to apply the knowledge gained in my chemistry courses and most recent field study to continue to enhance my geochemistry skills. The Chemistry Department's two-month summer excursion makes it one of the strongest in the world. I would excel greatly in this summer internship because of my analytical aptitude, drive for results, and proven success working in geochemistry teams.

The second semester of my freshman year in college, I was ranked number 1 in my chemistry class. As a result, in my sophomore year, I had the chance to serve as the chemistry professor's assistant in a freshman chemistry lab. Participating in a project led by my professor exposed me further to chemistry concepts, lab terminology, and most importantly, to the field of geochemistry. My professor invited me and a few other students to take a week-long field trip to an abandoned mine where we performed rock analysis. Our team presented our findings at the Annual Geochemistry Conference in Aspen earlier this year and received an award for our efforts.

The Chemistry Department's summer internship would provide me a chance to continue learning more about the geochemistry field. If selected, I am confident that my accomplishments in the Chemistry Department and within geochemistry in the last few years have given me a strong foundation. Please feel free to call me if you have further questions. Thank you for your consideration, and I look forward to your reply.

Sincerely,

LaConya Harris
3333 Conch Avenue
Miami, FL 77832
LaConya.Harris@mail.com
455-555-5555

Figure 17-3. Chemistry major's cover letter.

August 26, 2013

Dorothy Li, Recruiting Manager
Grover Sampson Consulting
2222 West Minister Street
New York, New York 44443

Dear Ms. Dorothy Li:

I am a senior political science major at the University of North Carolina at Chapel Hill and read about the social statistics associate opportunity in your company website's careers section. This position is important to me because it would give me working knowledge of how data can be used to influence political strategies. I was pleased to learn that Grover Sampson Consulting was recently ranked number 1 for employee satisfaction and number 1 for client success rate. My past experiences in analyzing large amounts of data, volunteering in two different political campaigns, and having the ability to learn quickly make me the perfect candidate for this role.

I became interested in political science during my freshman year when a friend and I decided to volunteer for Rebecca de la Cruz's city council campaign in Charlotte, North Carolina. I was primarily in charge of supporting the technology manager with the website and database. In addition, I assisted with data analysis of telecommunication costs associated with the campaign. De la Cruz's landslide victory motivated me to volunteer during my sophomore year for Dana Hillsworth's senatorial campaign in North Carolina. In this role, I supported the phone bank coordinator in ensuring that operations ran smoothly and learned a great deal about technology's impact on gaining more votes.

This position is ideal for me because it will allow me to gain experience in political strategy. I am a solid candidate for this role given my experience in data analysis and participation in campaign operations. Attached is my resume. Do not hesitate to contact me if you have any questions, and I hope you will consider me for the role. I look forward to hearing from you.

Thank you,

Jacob Ciglerski
6888 Mansfield Dam Street
Ashville, NC 33333
Jacob.Ciglerski@mail.com
999-999-9321

Figure 17-4. Political science major's cover letter.

Which Cover Letters Are the Most Effective? (IMPORTANT)

We just went through the structure of a cover letter and saw three samples. Now I have a question for you. Which of the three was the most effective? Was it the African studies major's, the chemistry major's, or the political science major's? Not sure? Please read on.

In the previous sections, we discussed that you should include in the introductory paragraph how you became familiar with the role. The African studies major indicated she became aware of the position through the African studies program's bulletin board. The chemistry major wrote that she found out about it through a professor, who also recommended that she apply. The political science major said he found out about the job through the company website's careers section. So which cover letter was the most effective?

> Your cover letter will be more effective if you indicate that you learned about the position from someone who works for the hiring company and that he or she encouraged you to apply.

All credentials being equal, hiring managers are more likely to hire applicants whom they know or whom their colleagues know. In this case, although all three cover letters were structurally correct, the chemistry major indicated she was encouraged to apply for the role by a professor in the Chemistry Department, the same department that is looking for a summer intern. The chemistry major had the most effective cover letter.

One of the easiest ways to meet someone who works for the company is to attend a networking event or a career fair. Here, a company representative may talk to you more about the role and even encourage you to apply, given your credentials. The next chapter discusses tips on how to make the most out of a career fair, so read on!

Chapter 18

Tips for Making the
Most Out of a Career Fair

One of the best places to distribute your resume is at a career fair, an event where recruiters seek talented individuals to fill available positions within their companies. Typically, it is held in a large space where each company has a booth and job seekers have the invaluable opportunity to network and increase their chances of getting an interview because of the personal interaction. However, many students make very serious mistakes that prevent them from getting the most out of the career fair experience. Below are several tips to assist you.

Always Arrive Early to the Career Fair (VERY IMPORTANT)

One of the biggest lessons I learned while at the university is that it is crucial to arrive early to a career fair, no later than fifteen minutes after the doors open. Why does being early pay off? First, many company recruiters will usually interview a certain number of people during the actual career fair if they feel they have strong candidates for a position they are trying to fill. However, once the interview time slots are full, no more interviews will be given there.

If you arrive late, you are decreasing your chances of getting an interview.

I remember one year, I went to two different career fairs that were hosted about two weeks apart. I arrived to the first about two hours before it was over and did not receive any interview offers. I arrived to the second one exactly when the doors opened. In the first hour, I spoke with four different companies, and three offered me an interview! Do you see my point?

Second, most career fairs can become very crowded. I remember once, I arrived to a career fair two hours after it began and had to wait in a thirty-minute line outside of the actual career fair before I was even able to go inside. Once in, it took me about forty-five minutes before I was able to speak to the first company representative!

If you arrive late, you may be standing in line for a long time until you are able to talk to a recruiter.

You may only have enough time to talk to one or two company representatives given how crowded career fairs can become.

Third, company recruiters get tired during this busy day. Imagine yourself talking to hundreds of students for several hours. After a while, everyone is going to start sounding the same and resumes looking alike.

If you want to make a strong impression, it is better to do so while the company recruiter is not exhausted from talking to different students all day.

To summarize, it is to your advantage to speak to a company recruiter earlier than later, so arrive early to the career fair.

Always Know Which Companies Will Be Present at the Career Fair

Many students tend to walk into a career fair not knowing which companies have sent recruiters. It is important you know which companies will be present before you even arrive so that you have time to research the different companies. You can determine which company representatives will be present by doing the following:

- Asking the career fair coordinator to provide you with a list of the companies
- Going to the career fair website to see what companies will be attending

Once you know which companies will have booths, at minimum, you should learn the following facts about each one:

- Company/industry's type (*e.g., oil & gas, financial services, telecommunications, health care*)
- Products or services provided (*e.g., computers, snacks, life insurance, flights*)
- Employment sites (*e.g., New York, San Francisco, Dallas, Miami, Brazil, China*)
- Number of employees (*e.g., twenty employees; fifty thousand employees; 260,000 employees*)
- Financial figures (*e.g., stock price, revenue and income generated last year/quarter*)
- Culture (*e.g., fast-paced, employee programs, employee benefits, company awards*)

Understanding companies' key characteristics will help you see if you are a good fit for them and whether you should approach their representatives at the career fair. You do not want to waste time speaking to recruiters you are not interested in when you can be speaking to those whom you want to work for as you may only have a short amount of time at the career fair to do so.

Do Not Ask Recruiters to Tell You What The Company Does. You Should Know Ahead of Time

When someone asks a recruiter what the company does, it sends an immediate red flag that the student did not do his or her homework. Company recruiters will be impressed if you have already done your research prior to approaching them because it will show that you are sure of what you are looking for.

What Do I Do if I Did Not Have Enough Time to Research All the Companies Prior to the Career Fair?

Sometimes there are so many companies at a career fair that we do not have enough time to research all of them prior to the day of the career fair. Also, there could be a situation where a company was not able to get its name on the career fair's website in time. If you see certain companies you may be interested in but know little about them, here are some recommendations:

- Do a quick two-minute research of a company using your smartphone while at the conference
- Before getting in line to speak to a representative, discreetly pick up a company brochure so you can read about the company as you wait in line.
- Ask friends at the conference to tell you a little bit about some of the companies they may have spoken with earlier at the conference.

Always Know Which Jobs Companies Are Looking to Fill Prior to the Day of the Career Fair

Just like knowing what a company does, it is important to know which jobs the recruiters are looking to fill prior to going to the career fair. This will give you a better idea of which ones you should approach. There are a few ways to determine what jobs the companies are looking to fill:

- Go to a particular company's website's careers section and perform a filter to narrow down any available jobs you may be interested in.
- Sometimes career fairs will have a career fair website where companies will post the jobs they are specifically looking to fill at the career fair. Make sure to check these out.
- Ask the career fair coordinator if the companies have listed their job postings.

Should I Apply for a Job That Is Posted on the Career Fair Website Prior to Going to the Career Fair?

Yes! If there is a job posted on the career fair website and you are qualified and interested in it, *always* apply for it prior to the day of the career fair. This may give you the opportunity to interview for the job or internship there. Imagine that! While everyone else is standing in line to speak to the company recruiters, you will be interviewing with them!

Bring Plenty of Resumes Inside a Folio

Make sure to bring enough general and job-specific resumes to hand out to the company recruiters and make sure to place them in a black folio to make sure they do not get wrinkled or dirty.

Be Prepared to Take Notes

You may want to bring a pen and paper to jot down any relevant information. For example, a company may ask you to interview a few days after the career fair, and you may want to have a pen available to write down a few notes.

Dress in Professional Attire

It is important that you look professional while at the career fair. Business casual is not recommended. Both men and women should wear suits and should stick to blacks, grays, and dark-blue colors. Being nicely groomed is important as well. When in doubt, just remember that dressing conservatively is the key.

Practice, Practice, Practice!

Talking to a recruiter may make you nervous. You may wonder, *What if they ask me a question and I say the wrong thing?* or *What if I forget the role I am interested in?* Don't panic. Prior to going to the career fair, it is beneficial to practice with a couple of friends or colleagues, alternating roles between the student and the recruiter by asking each other different questions. This will make you feel more comfortable once you are there.

Approaching a Company Recruiter

Remember, you should already know what the company does and what jobs it is looking to fill at the career fair. Once you are in front of the recruiter, I recommend the following procedure:

Step 1: Look at the company recruiter in the eyes and extend your hand to give him or her a *firm* handshake.

In a confident, conversational tone, say hi and give him or her the following information:

- Your first and last name
- The year in school you are in (e.g., freshman, sophomore, junior, senior)
- Your major
- The position you are interested in
- Where you learned about the position

Step 2: Tell the recruiter that you would like to provide him or her with your resume and gently hand it to him or her.

Step 3: Provide the recruiter with the top (two to three) reasons why you are qualified for the job/internship.

Below are a few examples of this three-step approach:

Example 1

"Hi, my name is Jill Doyle. I am a senior studying marketing at the University of Pennsylvania. I read about the business analyst position posted by [name of company] *on the career*

fair website and would like to discuss my qualifications with you and my reasons as to why I believe I would be a good fit for the role. Here is my resume for you to view. In my work experience section, you can see that I have experience in analyzing market trends and providing presentations to senior management."

Example 2

"Good morning, my name is Thomas Nguyen. I am a junior biochemistry major at Columbia University. I am interested in working in the pharmaceuticals industry, and I believe I am qualified for the research assistant role listed in your company's careers database. Here is a copy of my resume. In the summary of qualifications section, I provide you with a summary of my experiences with the necessary tools currently needed for the research assistant position. In addition, I have served in numerous leadership roles within my university, which have helped me develop my leadership and communication skills."

As you speak to the recruiter, don't be surprised if he or she chooses to spend a few seconds just reviewing your resume. He or she may ask you a few questions about its contents and relevant experiences. Make sure you speak as if you are having a conversation with him or her rather than as if you are reading a memorized script.

Once you are done speaking with the recruiter, he or she may ask you if you would be available to interview at the career fair. You should always be prepared for the interview, so I would recommend that you accept it rather than postpone it.

The recruiter may not ask you to be interviewed but inform you that he or she will hold on to your resume for further consideration. In this case, thank the recruiter for his or her time and ask for a business card. At this point, you are done and free to pick up additional company brochures at the booth.

Get the Recruiter's Business Card

It is not a bad idea to pick up business cards of company recruiters after speaking to them. Once at home, you can create a spreadsheet with companies and recruiters' names and their contact information. Please note that the spreadsheet will also come in handy if you attend other career fairs in the future because you will remember the recruiters' names if they happen to be there.

Send the Recruiter a Thank-You Letter

Sending the recruiter a thank-you letter will differentiate you from other potential candidates. After the career fair, I would recommend sending the letter through e-mail with the following information:

- Include a salutation using the same format described in the previous chapter.
- Thank them for giving you the opportunity to speak with them at the career fair.
- Reiterate your (two to three) reasons why you would be a good candidate for the role you are interested in.
- Demonstrate why you are interested in their company.
- Indicate that you look forward to their response.
- Attach your resume.

Fig. 18-1 is a good example of a thank-you e-mail to send a company recruiter.

Dear Mr. Parker:

Thank you for giving me the opportunity to speak with you at the Columbia University career fair about the research assistant role and my qualifications. I believe that my strong leadership skills and working knowledge of the required tools make me an ideal candidate for the position. Working for a company such as Vextra would be a rewarding experience given its track record as the most profitable and responsible pharmaceutical company in the country. Attached is my resume. Please feel free to contact me if you have any questions. I look forward to your reply.

Sincerely,

Thomas Nguyen
Box 343
2222 Tatalia Lane
New York, New York 77777
Thomas.Nguyen@mail.com
555-555-5555

Figure 18-1. Example of a thank-you e-mail.

In the next chapter, a final summary of tips for resume writing will be provided.

Chapter 19

Conclusion

As you prepare to finish writing your resume, review the general points covered in this book to make sure you have made use of all the major tips:

- The purpose of a resume is to get you an interview.
- Make sure your mailing address and phone number are up-to-date and that your e-mail address and voice mail look and sound professional.
- Your career objective should impart the following:

  o Explain what industry you want to work in and what position you want.
  o Use adjectives to describe your personal traits and skills.

- If your GPA is NOT 3.0 or higher, do NOT include it.
- Each item pertaining to your job descriptions should be in bullet format.
- Each bullet should begin with a verb.
- Quantify when possible.
- When you are explaining your job experiences, mention not only what you did but also what you learned, skills gained, and how you made a difference.
- Avoid acronyms.
- You do not need to describe everything you have done in a particular job, only what is most relevant.

- You do not need to include every job you have done in your life.
- Incorporate your technical and nontechnical skills into your job description bullets or in a separate section.
- Include awards, achievements, extracurricular activities, leadership roles, and additional languages spoken.
- If space permits, include community service events you have participated in, countries you have traveled to, special school projects you have completed, and hobbies you possess.
- Your resume should be no more than one page.
- One-inch margins should be used.
- Times New Roman and Arial are the preferred fonts, and the letter size should be between 10 and 12.
- Headers stand out in the resume when making them bold, italicized, and/or underlined.
- 60 percent of the paper making up the resume should be filled with words and 40 percent should be the white space of the paper.
- Make sure there are no misspellings or grammar errors.
- Always attach your resume as a PDF file when e-mailing it to a recruiter.

So what's next? After completing your resume, you will make changes to it every four to six months as you gain more skills, work experiences, and accomplishments. However, choose to modify your resume sooner if you are applying for a new position in the near future.

*   *   *

Writing a resume without any direction can be an exhausting experience. I hope that reading this book has made your resume-writing exercise easy and that the tips on creating a cover letter and making the most out of a career fair were helpful. I have had the opportunity to mentor many friends and colleagues on resume writing and enjoy their high satisfaction once a session is over and a winning resume has been created.

As you embark on your journey to enter the job market, having an exceptional resume will always take you further and make you more confident about yourself. I am a firm believer that we are all great at something. We all possess unique strengths useful to society, and it is our responsibility to use them to improve the world we live in. Life is about becoming successful and helping others become successful as well.

Maya Angelou, renowned American author and poet, said,

"When you learn, teach. When you get, give."

Use this opportunity to learn as much as you can and share or teach this knowledge to others. Strive to be happy in your life and always find a way to give happiness back.

I want to wish you the best of luck with your resume and in your career. Congrats to you for taking the extra time and effort to read this book. You are now several steps ahead of your competition and ready to pursue your career goals, accompanied by a new ally, a very powerful and loyal one, which will support you during your job hunting days—a resume that stands out!

Index

**Schedule your next group session or seminar today with
The Resume Whiz™!**

L. Xavier Cano is known as ***The Resume Whiz***™ for his 100% track record of placing his clients into jobs in 4 weeks or fewer and is one of America's leading resume writing and career coaches for college students and recent graduates.

Xavier graduated summa cum laude from the University of Houston with a degree in industrial engineering in 2004 where he was named the University of Houston Scholar & Leader of the Year. He received his MBA from the University of Texas at Austin in 2010 where he received a full tuition fellowship from The Consortium. Xavier is a certified Project Management Professional (PMP), certified Green Belt in Six Sigma, and has held roles within Continental Airlines, Frito-Lay, Dell, Cipher Business Solutions, and Bank of America.

"When asked why I enjoy coaching others on resume writing, I say that it is because of the satisfaction I receive from observing the self-confidence that grows within those I help."

—*The Resume Whiz*™

Book your next group session or seminar with *The Resume Whiz*™ today by visiting www.theinnovativeresume.com.

CPSIA information can be obtained at www.ICGtesting.com
Printed in the USA
LVOW04s1459180615

442982LV00018B/919/P